Your Dream Job Game Plan

5 tools for becoming your own career agent

Top female sports agent

Molly Fletcher

with Steve Kincaid

Molly Fletcher

GO FOR IT!

Your Dream Job Game Plan

© 2009 by Molly Fletcher
Published by JIST Works, an imprint of JIST Publishing
7321 Shadeland Station, Suite 200
Indianapolis, IN 46256-3923
Phone: 800-648-JIST   Fax: 877-454-7839   E-mail: info@jist.com

Visit our Web site at **www.jist.com** for information on JIST, free job search tips, tables of contents, sample pages, and ordering instructions for our many products!

Trade Product Manager: Lori Cates Hand
Cover Designer: Mike Bailey
Interior Designers: Aleata Halbig, Toi Davis
Page Layout: Toi Davis
Proofreaders: Paula Lowell, Jeanne Clark
Indexer: Kelly D. Henthorne

Printed in the United States of America
13 12 11 10 09   9 8 7 6 5 4 3 2

    Library of Congress Cataloging-in-Publication Data
Fletcher, Molly, 1971-
    Your dream job game plan : five tools to becoming your own career agent / Molly Fletcher ; with Steve Kincaid.
        p. cm.
    Includes index.
    ISBN 978-1-59357-612-7 (alk. paper)
  1. Career development. 2. Job hunting. I. Kincaid, Steve (Stephen B.) II. Title.
    HF5381.F64 2009
    650.14--dc22

                                2008036560

ISBN 978-1-59357-612-7

CONTENTS

ACKNOWLEDGMENTS

I didn't have a book like this in mind when I packed up and moved from East Lansing, Michigan, to Atlanta, Georgia. I was an unemployed college graduate hoping to secure my dream job in the business of sports, but had no plans to be an author. But as I became aware of the value of my experience, the idea for this book began to come together. A lot of special people supported my vision. I am very appreciative of their love and assistance.

Of course, I must start with my partner in life—my best friend—my husband, Fred Fletcher. Fred is an awesome and special man. He has tremendous character, a great style about him, and is likable to all. Much of my vision for this book crystallized in the first years following the birth of our three children, all born within 13 months. Without Fred's support of my passion to share this philosophy with young adults, this book would not have happened.

I was blessed to have parents, Mary and Ken West, who have always believed in me. They never told me anything was impossible. They told me things might be tough and I might have to work very hard, but they always told me it was *possible*. They knew exactly when to push me hard and exactly when to hug me. They mentored me not only with their words but with their actions. My mom and dad are two of the most respectful, classy, and giving people I know. They are individuals to emulate while being a perfect couple as well. Their approach and philosophy to parenting is one I try to duplicate with our own children. They are and will forever be my greatest mentors and my heroes.

My twin brothers, Jim and John West, treated me like a little brother, not a little sister. They made me gutsy and a little tough. They taught me if I wanted to jump into the pile of leaves and wrestle with them, I could—but I might get hurt and couldn't come crying when I did. There was no easy road growing up in a home with twin brothers, five years older. And to this day, I thank them for the toughness they instilled in me and the love they have for their "little sister."

Thank you to Lonnie Cooper, CEO and Founder of Career Sports & Entertainment, for giving me an opportunity. Lonnie taught me much of what I know from a professional perspective. His stellar reputation, impeccable communication skills, and awesome style are marvelous. He cares deeply about his clients and his employees and I owe my professional success to him. I've studied him and I've learned from him. He showed me how to embrace opportunities and challenges. He taught me how to manage up and manage down. He provided me with the platform to start my career and the nurturing to flourish as a sports agent and an executive.

Of course, thank you to Steve Kincaid for all his energy and effort. His education, insights, and professional experiences have added great value to this project, and his commitment to my vision helped me define, articulate, and shape my ideas. Finally, I want to again thank the hundreds of people who spent time with me when I asked for advice. I was young and eager but still learning to channel my passion. I even want to thank those who never called me back, and the many people who told me I had "no chance" when I shared my vision of pursuing a career in the business of sports. You motivated me, and now you are helping me motivate others. Thank you to the young people I've met with over the years. Each of you has helped me crystallize this five-tool formula and now, with the help of this book, we can influence others who have a vision for building their own dream careers, too.

Introduction

I love my job. I want you to be able to say that, too.

As one of a handful of female sports agents in the United States, I love the challenges and opportunities I face every day. Career Sports & Entertainment, Inc., our agency, currently represents more than 200 of the most recognizable names in baseball, coaching, golf, and broadcasting. We manage relationships for them with their teams, universities, sponsors, and networks. We initiate new opportunities and we are their greatest advocates. We maximize their passion for their sport. We channel their confidence and fearlessness both on and off the field. Together, we develop and execute a lifelong game plan relevant to their careers on the field and beyond. We help them create choices for themselves. And of course, we negotiate on their behalf. Most important, we help build and enhance our clients' brands.

Why I Love My Job

Why do I love my job? I embrace the relationship-building side of my work, whether it's with the clients, their employers, their families, or our colleagues in the office. Managing relationships with people who have reached the elite level of their craft requires that I become a friend, a sister, and a confidant. I am their most consistent and reliable advocate. For me to be successful, I have to be one of the few people in their world that will be fully honest with them.

With this many clients, someone's life is changing at any given moment. Athletes have a very limited window of opportunity to use their skills, and we have to maximize it. Our clients win, they sometimes lose, they set records, they get hired, they get fired, they speak to the media, they are approached with good and bad opportunities for us to filter—it never stops. We need to anticipate their next career opportunities and their challenges, and we must react to each of them quickly.

I love the uniqueness of my job. Because many people find my business intriguing, I am often asked to speak to companies, and at universities and events throughout the country. My message and my stories depend on my audience—be it speaking on leadership, motivation, pursuing your dreams, work-life-balance, overcoming challenges, or a plethora of other topics. The one most relevant to this book is when I speak to people either attempting to secure their first job or starting down the paths to their own dream career.

When I speak to young people, I teach that you can secure great jobs by being consistently, uniquely, and respectfully persistent. This often means being different from friends and trying a different approach to finding great jobs. After I speak, I find that about 100 people out of every 1,000 will approach me to ask additional questions or talk further. I am happy to try to help, and welcome them to e-mail me or my assistant if they are interested in additional advice. I recall the challenges of fulfilling my own passion and the numerous people who helped me do so. I feel it's now my responsibility to do the same for others like you.

Out of the 100 people who approach me after a speech, I find only 30 ever follow up. Four or five will do so within a few hours of walking out of the room, and the rest do so over the next week or two.

Of those who send an initial e-mail, only two or three will make the effort to stay in touch with me—to build a relationship.

Of course, it is this small group of persistent networkers that gets my attention. Within a relatively short period of time, I come to feel like I know them. I'm sure they feel the same—they have a contact and a resource in the industry. So although lots of people approach me for help, it seems only 2 to 3 percent "get it" and understand how to be their own agent.

Connecting into Your First Job

Many of you reading this book are beginning to think about entering the working world or are early in your career and thinking of a transition to your true passion. You probably have all kinds of hopes, ambitions, and goals. Armed with your education, a few contacts, and your enthusiasm, you're ready to conquer the world and make your mark. You probably have a dream career in mind, one that is challenging but difficult to obtain. Maybe it's one that gets you excited about going in on Mondays and disappointed when you have to go home on Fridays. Maybe it is a six-figure package (that has the potential to become a two-comma salary). Maybe it's the corner office on the top floor. Whatever it is, you think of it as the dream career in your field.

Hopefully, it's a job you feel passionate about. Surveys (like those done by the National Association of Colleges and Employers) usually show that the single most important criteria to young people when choosing a career and employer is the *enjoyment of the work*. You want to have what organizational psychologists call "high job satisfaction"; you want to be excited by your work, you want to feel engaged, and you want to be happy.

Let's say you are the typical American worker. You connect with your first professional job out of college at age 22. Then you work between 40 and 50 hours a week, 50 weeks a year (you do take time off for vacation, right?) for the next 43 years, until you are about 65 years old. That means that over the course of your career, you will have spent more than 100,000 hours at work! Don't you want to spend all this time doing work you love and that feels important?

Unfortunately, I see so many people who have realized that a college degree itself is no guarantee of playing in the big leagues. Statistics show that more and more people graduate from college every year, and that this trend will continue into the future. This tells you that more young people will look for dream careers than there are dream careers to be found. I am familiar with this personally. In most sports, there are more agents than there are athletes to represent. It's no surprise that I see so many young people discouraged as they try to join the work force. Many will have to take jobs that are less exciting than they had hoped.

Of course, those who land in less exciting jobs often have not put in the extra effort needed to pursue their dream careers. To me, it seems their only effort is to "hope" they can connect with the right company and the right job. When I meet with people, I can quickly size up the people who are building their professional lives on hope. I hear them talk about how other people have "caught a break" or "gotten lucky." When I hear this, I always disagree with them about what luck really is. Luck is putting yourself in a position to take advantage of the opportunities you create. Luck is where perseverance and preparation meet an opportunity. You must create your own luck. Luck takes work.

Creating Your Luck

Because I work in the sports business, I pay attention to the way people talk about athletes and have noticed that some people talk about the differences between "elite" athletes and everybody else. It's as if they think there is a huge talent difference between the #1 guy on the PGA Tour

Money List and the #70 guy, or between a future Hall of Famer and the third pitcher in his team's rotation. The gap isn't as big as you might think.

Did you know pro baseball teams are allowed to carry only 25 people on their opening-day rosters? Add up all the rosters of all the American League and National League teams and you'll find there is room for only 750 baseball players in the big leagues. If you include all the players on all the rosters of the 246 minor-league teams, you'll find you have another 6,000 or so players. Some are on their way up, some are on their way down, and some are on their way out of the game. Every player in pro baseball—at any level—is already the best of the best.

Yes, it's easy to think the difference between the best in the big leagues and the rest is luck. In the movie *Bull Durham,* Crash Davis talks about the difference between a minor-league player and one who gets the chance to play in the majors:

> *Know what the difference between hitting .250 and .300 is? It's 25 hits. Twenty-five hits in 500 at bats [over a season] is 50 points, okay? There's 6 months in a season, that's about 25 weeks. That means if you get just one extra flare a week, just one—a gorp, you get a groundball, you get a "groundball with eyes," you get a dying quail, just one more dying quail a week—and you're in Yankee Stadium.*

Some of the pros are clearly bigger, stronger, and faster than other players. But what about the rest? How did they get to the big leagues? How did they stand out? They created the opportunity for themselves to play at this level. They were disciplined. Although they had to have the talent, they weren't afraid of a lot of hard work. They tried to create an opportunity for themselves by doing the extra things that set the very best apart from the rest. They pushed themselves harder. They took the extra at-bats. They ran the extra laps. They hit the weight room, and they avoided life's distractions.

You can see this same determination in people outside of sports, too. Thomas Edison made more than 1,000 attempts at inventing a functional electric light before finding that one key to success. He had a creativity that sustained him, that let him envision and try multiple approaches. He took the perspective that he didn't fail 999 times; he learned 999 ways not to make a light bulb! Henry Ford went bankrupt four times before starting a successful company, but he didn't let fear keep him from trying again. And, as Crash Davis said, a big-league player has to be successful only 30 percent of the time to be one of the best hitters on the team.

A Look Behind the Curtain

I know that you have hopes, ambitions, and goals for your career, but your road map might not be clear. Now, with 15 years of experience in the working world and having earned what some would call a dream job, I want to help. I want to increase that 2 to 3 percent of people who really understand how to pursue and secure the right career to a much larger percentage. If I can increase the proportion who "get it," I can also help increase the proportion of you who reach your career goals. And on the most basic level, I can help ensure that more people have the unique opportunity to wake up every day and be excited about what they do.

Have you seen *The Wizard of Oz*? Do you remember the scene where Toto pulls back the curtain to reveal that the wizard is a man pulling all the levers and pushing all the buttons? I am going to take you behind the curtain and show you how to get a dream career. No one explains this to you when you are in your twenties, and it might look like magic, but once you understand the process of how things really work, once you look behind the curtain, everything becomes much clearer. I'll show you what it takes to set yourself apart from everybody else. That's why I wrote this book.

I am going to make this process fun for you. I know looking for a job is hard work and can be very stressful. I want to teach you what all the books, all the Web sites, and all the career guides don't. If you believe your resume and a cover letter will find you a dream job, be prepared to change that belief. But if you want me to take you behind the curtain, keep reading. I will explain how the process of finding the dream jobs really works.

Because these ideas are so important, I've asked a good friend, Dr. Steve Kincaid, to bring his expertise and point of view into the mix. Steve is a corporate psychologist and a consultant in a top-tier firm that works with the biggest companies and private equity firms in the world. He has spent his career working to help business executives reach their goals and organizations identify the best candidates for critical roles. Like me, he loves his job. Both of us feel so fortunate to be in careers we enjoy so much. Whenever the elevator doors open for me at Career Sports & Entertainment, Inc., and whenever Steve heads to the airport to fly off to meet with a client or interview candidates for a CEO position, we are happy, excited, and proud of what we do and who we represent. But these jobs weren't just handed to us. We worked for them and were careful in the choices we made.

Over the years, I have watched a lot of bright and talented young people make mistakes in the job search process. It saddens me, because I see many of them have what it takes to be successful, but they make mistakes that lead them to miss some great opportunities. As a result, I wrote this book, and wanted Steve to add his insight.

As you read this book, you will see that it's about five tools you must master to best position yourself to pursue your dream career. I have tried to include as many step-by-step guides to my philosophy and approach as possible so that you can capture and apply what I have learned over my years in the highly competitive work world of professional sports. This book teaches you what *really matters* in starting your own career. I'll give you examples, tell you stories of people just like you who have done the right things (and a few who have done the wrong things), and I will help you build a roadmap of your own. You will learn how to build relationships with people who can help you, whether or not you know them now. And when you land that great offer, I will help you with your negotiations and help you set yourself up for a positive start in your new career.

We're not in Kansas anymore—at times, it will be hard work, but stay disciplined and passionate. I'm excited to guide you on this journey! I've tried to make my ideas as practical and realistic as possible. Together we'll start you on the way to being a star in your dream career.

Let's go get it!

My Story

CHAPTER 1

The Two Questions You Must Be Able to Answer

I don't know you, but I know what you want.

You want a great job and to build a great career. You want to love your work so much that it really isn't "work." You want to wake up every morning and be excited about what you do. You want to get paid what you are worth. You want to feel valued and appreciated for what you bring to the job.

I know you want this, because it is was what I wanted, too. Fortunately, I've learned what you need to know.

Two years after graduating from Michigan State University, I found myself in Atlanta, sitting in the office of Lonnie Cooper. Lonnie started and built a successful company called Career Sports & Entertainment, Inc., and I had come seeking his advice on how to start a career in the business of sports. Like most college students, I had come to this meeting with a well-written and concise resume that I thought captured my assets and highlighted the accomplishments of my academic, athletic, and short professional career. Like most twenty-somethings, I sat down, made some small talk, scooted my resume across his desk to him, and waited for him to start asking questions about my degree, my background, and my GPA.

But Lonnie didn't do that. He was not like everybody else who had taken the time to meet with me. Instead of asking the usual questions I had been expecting, Lonnie briefly looked down at my resume, looked up again at me, and then proceeded to crumple up my resume and shoot it into the trash can across the room. Then he asked me two simple but central questions:

Molly, who are you? And what do you want to do?

To make it to the big leagues in your field—whether that field is finance, science, medicine, education, or anything else—you have to ask and answer these questions of yourself. If you can answer these with clarity and confidence, finding your dream career will become much, much easier.

Today, more than ten years after Lonnie asked me these questions, I am President of Career Sports & Entertainment, Inc. I have what many people would consider a dream job: I am a sports agent, and one of only a few women working among the thousands of registered sports agents in the United States. We represent more than 200 clients, many of whom you know well. Finding my way to Lonnie's office wasn't easy, but it wasn't impossible. Finding your way to your dream career won't be easy either, but you can do it. Let me tell you my story.

My Dream Job

Early in my college years, I realized that I wanted to work in the business of sports. I was an athlete and played tennis at Michigan State University. But I had a limited understanding of the business of sports, what kinds of opportunities existed, and whether my own strengths, weaknesses, and background would help me succeed.

Introspection and Investigation

I began by thinking through my interests. On the most basic level, I knew that I enjoyed people and I enjoyed building relationships. I knew that I loved fixing problems and finding solutions. I knew that I wanted to help others be happy and "take care of them." I knew I wanted to turn adversarial situations into win-win solutions. I had a clear sense of my passion and a crystallizing view of how my strengths would be an asset to help me capitalize on my interests.

As I thought about my strengths, I started to realize that managing relationships within the sports industry was a role that fit me well. I didn't really understand what jobs this realization meant I should pursue, but it was a start.

Throughout college, I kept my eyes and ears open, trying to learn all I could and refine my vision. I started talking about my vision to friends and family. Some gave me motivational advice, and some didn't. One of the things I learned was that jobs in the sports business are difficult to secure—many people even told me they were "inaccessible." Some told me being a top-tier and successful sports agent, especially as a female, was as tough as becoming a professional athlete. In fact, I sat in front of people who looked me straight in the eyes and told me "the business is too competitive—you'll never get a job in sports." Others told me, "I always wanted to do that as well, but it's impossible." Never did their negative words trigger a little voice inside of me trying to say "they're right—you can't do it."

The Search Was On

I tried everything I could think of to get a job that would build toward a career in the sports business. I started just like everybody else. I polished my resume and wrote professional cover letters. I sent them to people whom I didn't know and who didn't know me. I responded to ads in the paper (we didn't have the Internet then). I became the typical "college graduate without a job," putting lots of lines in the water and hoping someone would take notice of me and bite. I got some nibbles, but nobody would take the bait and start me on the road to the dream career I wanted.

As I came to the end of my college years, I began to realize that a direct-mail, mass-marketing approach wasn't working. I recognized that *people* hire people, and that my resume was probably one of hundreds, if not thousands, sent in response to any given ad. As I thought about it, I realized that I didn't have the relationships I needed to even get on the radar screen of anyone in the sports industry. I realized I would have to build more relationships, and *more effective* relationships with the right people. Although I didn't know it then, I made a decision that was the start of putting into practice what has become the philosophy behind this book. I realized that if I wanted my dream job, I couldn't expect for it to come to me. I had to pursue it—and pursue it daily.

The Big Step That Started It All

My pursuit started when I took my life savings of $2,000 out of the bank and moved from East Lansing, Michigan, to Atlanta, Georgia. Atlanta was not a random choice. During the 1990s, Atlanta was becoming one of the centers of the sports universe. The Braves had completed their worst-to-first miracle season and the start of their unprecedented run of consecutive divisional titles. The Super Bowl was coming to town, and preparations for the 1996 Olympics were consuming every corner of the city. The city was fast becoming a sports hub, and I hoped it would have a place for me. In 1993, I arrived in a little green Honda Accord packed to the brim with everything I owned—even my bike!

But in and among all my worldly belongings, the most valuable possessions I brought to Atlanta were the names of two people I thought might be able to help me, even though I had never met them. These two people weren't in the sports marketing business, but they helped me along the path that led to my first sports marketing job. I had their names because people who liked me enough to want to help me had made an introduction for me. When I got to Atlanta, I reached out to these two, met with them, and asked for advice. I was able to get them to want to help me. They agreed to introduce me to people they knew. This was the way I began taking my first steps toward meeting people in the business of sports. You have people like this in your life, too, and later I'm going to show you how to identify and get in front of the people who can help you.

Before I moved to Atlanta, I started learning the names of all the important people in the Atlanta world of sports. Of course, there were the professional teams—the Braves, the Hawks, and the Falcons (the Thrashers weren't in Atlanta yet). I had learned all the key players involved with the Olympics and the Super Bowl, the two areas I thought gave me my best shot for breaking into the business. I also found out about The Atlanta Sports Council, an organization that hosts monthly "networking" sessions. I attended my first meeting just days after I arrived in Atlanta. Because of my research, I knew that Leeman Bennett (the former head coach of the Falcons, Atlanta's football team) was the Executive Director of the Super Bowl Host Committee, and regularly attended the Atlanta Sports Council meetings.

At my first ASC meeting, I sought out Leeman in a room full of people. Leeman is a tall, broad-shouldered, and powerful-looking man who has the confident appearance of a professional athlete and a successful coach. It would have been easy to be intimidated. I wasn't. I went up to him and introduced myself to him. I said "Coach, you must be enjoying preparing for Super Bowl XXVIII. Congrats on bringing this to Atlanta. What an honor for the city. I just graduated from Michigan State and would love to spend 15 minutes with you to get your thoughts and advice on breaking into the sports marketing business in Atlanta." When I finished, I found he was welcoming and encouraging, and he agreed. We made plans to meet later that week at his office.

What a productive meeting! After I spent time asking him for advice and learning as much as I could about how the sports business really worked, Leeman asked me if I would be interested in an entry-level opportunity with him. "Yes, of course I would," I said! At that, he offered me a job with the Super Bowl Host Committee. Now, don't get too excited yet. This job was definitely *not* in the big leagues. I answered phones in the office of the Super Bowl Host Committee. But I knew it was a great opportunity for me to get a taste of sports marketing for one of the biggest events on the planet. I also knew that, even though the Super Bowl itself would come and go very quickly, it was a great opportunity for me to meet the key sports executives in town.

Early Career Moves

Although you might say I only answered the phones, I had the chance to speak with Paul Tagliabue, the commissioner of the NFL. I spoke with the Vice President of Marketing for Coke, key executives at Home Depot, and leaders of BellSouth. I could go on and on. What I knew was that this job really offered me the chance to create a dialogue with key sports busi nesspeople in Atlanta. I realized that if I could form relationships with these people—somehow—that I would be much, much closer to starting my career.

After the Super Bowl, I was out of work again. Because I knew that relationships were more powerful than resumes, I realized that I needed to continue to find ways to meet people with connections, whether they were in the sports business or outside it. I was facing a gap in full-time work. So I took a part-time position with a company called Executive Adventures, taking corporate executives through team-building exercises, so that I could build relationships. Even though I was afraid of heights, I started working high rope courses. This wasn't because I thought rope courses were relevant to getting into sports management. I did it in order to gain valuable team-building experiences and also to meet people who could help me. All the major corporations in town were sending executives through the program, and I knew I would be able to expand my network of contacts in Atlanta.

As I got to know the executives who came through our program, I waited for the appropriate time and then asked whether I could meet with them outside the rope course to gain their advice on my career goals. At the same time, I was continuing to tap into relationships I had made during my time at the Super Bowl. Between my relationships from the Super

Bowl and Executive Adventures, I secured informational meetings with executives from Chick-fil-A, Coca-Cola, and UPS, just to name a few. Some of these companies had sports-marketing functions and some didn't. I used these meetings to truly seek advice on building a career I was passionate about, but also to gain referrals. I'll tell you more about how you can capitalize and leverage meetings like this in later chapters. But for now, you should know that asking one executive for advice often led me to an introduction to another executive.

Eventually I uncovered awesome job opportunities. Some were in sports and some weren't. On one hand, at UPS they wanted me to join their management training program. On the other hand, the executives I gained access to at Chick-fil-A wanted me to consider working in the sponsorship side of the business. I have to say, I was tempted to take the position at Chick-fil-A because they are a fantastic company built on important life values, but the day-to-day duties of the position were not ones I could be passionate about. I let both opportunities pass.

Over time, my money began to run out. Eventually, it became the bottom of the ninth for me. The pressure was on, but I persevered. Each and every day, I woke up and followed my game plan that I knew would help me work toward my goal. I carefully maintained the relationships I had built and continued to find ways to build new relationships. Day after day, I did research, read about the sports business, made phone calls, and respectfully tapped into my contacts. I created great reasons to call people I had met with, and I ensured that the people I was networking with knew my commitment.

I aggressively attended sports-management conferences to expand my relationship base. I scoured the Atlanta market for executives in sports marketing. I listened carefully to any advice I was given. But most of all, I continued to believe in myself and embrace my dream. As a result, my database of names kept growing.

Another Step Closer

One of my informal meetings was with the CEO of Intellimedia Sports, Inc., a licensee of ESPN. Ben Dyer, the CEO, had started the company by creating and selling instruction CD-ROMs. Intellimedia was in the early stages of distributing these instructional CD-ROMs across the country. The company secured some of the biggest names in their sports at the time to host the videos.

I remember sitting on the edge of my seat in a one-on-one meeting with Mr. Dyer. I had dressed the part (I had one or maybe two nice business suits) and I had my leather notebook. But the most important thing I had was my passionate style and fearlessness. I was prepared; I knew the CD-ROMs they had produced so far and I had worked to gather information on their plans for future CD-ROMs. I even visited a few of the sporting-goods stores in Atlanta to see whether they were distributed in large stores yet.

I had done my research. And although this was "just an informational meeting," I wanted to work for Mr. Dyer and be a part of growing Intellimedia. My gut (and that is all it was as I hadn't spoken to anyone at the company nor did I understand their structure) told me to try for a role on their sales side.

But truth be told, I was young and inexperienced.

As we talked, I remember telling him, "I am a former student-athlete who knows how to work hard, who knows how to do a little more to be a little better. I understand discipline. I want to win; I understand teamwork because I've been a part of teams all my life. And, certainly, I have a passion to work in the business of sports. But, Mr. Dyer, what does that all mean and really matter to you and Intellimedia?"

"I want to and will have (said softly with a very humble smile) an impact on revenue for a company. I want to be a part of a growing company beside great people who have tremendous passion. Most of all, I want to work for a company with a CEO with a great reputation. I've done my research. Intellimedia is all of those things and more."

He would have to bet on me. And, he did. I started in 1994 selling the CD-ROMs to small sporting-goods stores all over the country. But Intellimedia was suffocating because of the Internet boom and the CD-ROM business was beginning to really struggle. It was soon time for me to move on. Because of my few years of relentless scouring, good meetings, and appropriate follow-up, I had a fairly expansive stack of business cards. I had met someone at a sports-marketing conference a few years back whom I thought could help me. She was in a career that didn't really interest me, but she was sharp and impressive. I reached out to her and asked whether I could buy her a cup of coffee and get her advice as I looked to transition into another area of the sports business. Although she wasn't in sports, I knew she was smart and successful, and probably knew some people she could connect me to.

After years of informational interviews, I had gotten pretty good at networking meetings. During the meeting, I felt we connected, so toward the end of the meeting I asked her whether there were other people she thought would be helpful for me to meet. She referred me to three more people she knew, which led me to someone at a place called Career Sports.

The Big Opportunity

I called the person at Career Sports and asked the same question I asked every referral:

> *May I meet with you to get your advice on securing a job in the sports business as well as learn more about future growth plans inside Career Sports & Entertainment?*

He was agreeable, and we had a very productive meeting. Within the first five minutes, I made sure he knew I was passionate and well prepared for this meeting. I had done my research. I asked great questions about the existing business and his thoughts on the growth of the agency, as well as more global questions about niches in the sports business. After about 30 minutes, he said "You know, you should really meet Lonnie, our CEO. We might need someone like you one day." Now I was excited!

That afternoon I contacted Lonnie and secured time on his calendar. A week later, I found myself sitting in Lonnie's office, watching him crumple up my carefully crafted resume and asking me exactly who I was and what I wanted to do.

Answering the Critical Questions

As I watched Lonnie throw my resume into the trash can, I thought that this was not what any book I had read on finding a career had prepared me for. I had come in expecting to give my typical speech about my three strengths and my three weaknesses (which I would cleverly reveal to actually be strengths). I was caught off guard when Lonnie asked me who I was and what I wanted to do because he was asking me a much deeper, more important, and fundamental set of questions. Today, I know that his questions are where you must start when working toward your own dream career. "Who are you? And what do you want to do?" are *the* critical questions you must be able to answer. And you have to convey your answers in a way that helps you stand out from everybody else.

When Lonnie asked me these questions, a nervous shock ran through me, but I quickly embraced the heart of his questions. On one level, I tried to answer in a way that showed Lonnie my passion. I told him, "I want to work in the business of sports for a well-respected and reputable company. I want to work in an environment that encourages growth for its employees and welcomes creative thinking. I want to work with a group of people who get excited about today's success but more excited about how that success translates into tomorrow's opportunities for growth. I want to be rewarded appropriately for my contributions to that growth. And I want to be a part of building something very, very special."

On a more subtle level, I also tried to communicate what I believed would be important to him as the CEO of a growing sports agency, saying "It is important to me to align with an agency that has an outstanding reputation." I had done my research, and Career Sports had an outstanding reputation. That was and is important to me. At some point in the meeting, I also said with a humbly respectful but confident tone, "You have an impressive client list, but there is a lot more business out there. The competition locally is irrelevant and it seems this agency can be the leader in the Southeast and the nation and, in time, internationally."

As you will find is often the case with many successful businesspeople, the fact that I had *created* this opportunity to sit in front of the CEO of a successful sports agency communicated quite a bit to Lonnie about me. Lonnie indicated he was intrigued with my ability to contribute to the agency on the representation side of the business and asked me to follow up 60 days later with his "right-hand person," who was out on maternity leave. So exactly 60 days later—and in fact, at exactly nine in the morning on day 60—I called and set up a second meeting. This second meeting was scheduled for just 30 minutes, but three and a half hours later, I came out of what had been an incredibly positive discussion. Just hours later, I was offered a job—a chance—with Career Sports & Entertainment. I had earned my chance to play in the big leagues.

I have made the most of this opportunity and have been a part of building this business into something unique and well respected. Now, I'm going to ask you the same questions Lonnie asked me:

Who are you? And what do you want to do?

These are the most important questions. Once you can answer them, you are ready to begin applying the rest of my approach for getting your own chance in the big leagues. This will require hard work, but it is not impossible. As you read, you will see that my philosophy is that you must pay close attention to two things:

- What you are doing in your job search

- How you are doing it

What to do?

- First, use your relationships, not your resume.

- Second, get people to like and respect you enough to want to help you or hire you.

How do you do this?

By asking for advice, not for a job.

This simple philosophy—although it's hard work to implement—is how you will close the relationship gap that stands between you and your dream career.

Wrapping Up and Moving On

Now you've heard the basics of my story and the most important questions you must be able to answer. Are you prepared to answer the two most important questions?

CHAPTER 2

How the Job Market Really Works: The Relationship Gap Between You and Your Dream Job

If you look around and you are doing things differently from everybody else, you're probably doing it right. If you think you are being too aggressive, you probably aren't. If you think you are meeting too many people, you aren't. Trust me: Each meeting is getting you closer to the person who is going to hire you.

The truth is that people hire people; people don't hire paper! This means you must get in front of people and get them excited about you. It's that simple. Get them to like you. Create reasons through awesome and healthy dialogue for people to feel like they need you and that you will add value to their business.

This chapter is about the relationship gap between you and your dream job—and how to close it.

An Opportunity to Close the Gap

I joined Career Sports & Entertainment in 1996, when the firm was 10 years old. In 1998, one of our clients, George Lombard, was a highly touted dual-sport athlete coming out of a private school in Atlanta. As a hometown hero, George was fortunate enough to be drafted by the Atlanta Braves in the second round. George was a very polished and classy young man whose mother died when he was young. In some ways, I felt like I was a mother figure in his life. He and I would speak almost daily, about everything from his swing to his batting stance to his dinner plans and his family and friends. I would often visit George at spring training or in the different minor-league cities throughout the season, and sometimes when I visited I would join George in the gym for a workout.

It was on a Saturday morning during one of my visits that I found myself in the gym with George and his friend Wes Helms, another promising prospect in the Braves organization, and someone we believed would fit well with our agency. Wes had already signed with another agency. I was very familiar with Wes and his potential because I had been tracking his progress since he was drafted, but I had never met him. Many of our clients were friends with Wes, and I knew he had a tremendous reputation and was also well respected in the game. Of course, I had always wanted to meet him and took this chance to congratulate him on several of his accomplishments.

After George introduced us and we began to talk, I casually congratulated him on some of his stats and his pace of progress through the minor leagues. He seemed surprised that I was aware of some of these specifics—maybe because he was a minor-league player, maybe because we didn't represent him, or maybe because I was a woman. Toward the end of the workout, I had an idea on how to continue to build our relationship. I asked Wes if he would be interested in joining some of our other clients as part of a camp we had created for young kids in Atlanta. We find our clients often enjoy hosting baseball camps as a way to "give back" to the community as well as help young kids, and I saw this as a means to find a positive reason to stay in contact with Wes. He was very interested, so I got his e-mail and phone number.

I certainly wanted to grow our client base with the right kind of guys, and now that I had met Wes I knew he was just that kind of guy. But I also knew that I first had to continue to build our relationship while I determined whether our capabilities as an agency would match up with his goals. I knew I could build our relationship by remaining very aware of and attentive to his world. I knew the camp gave me the perfect reason to stay in contact with him. So the afternoon of the same day I had met him, I e-mailed him, letting him know what a pleasure it was to meet him after hearing about him from George (and others) for so many years.

Then, over the next several weeks, I continued to communicate with him regarding the logistics and various details pertaining to the camp. Every time I contacted him, I would congratulate him on something that I knew was relevant to him. I also began to discuss recent team signings to show him that I was "in his world" from the baseball viewpoint as well. When it came time to discuss the minute details of the camp, like where he needed to park and the sponsors' roles, I also found a way to let him know I was tracking his career by asking a question or two on where he was hitting in the order or a recent trade the Braves had made. At the same time, I was showing him how Career Sports & Entertainment handles marketing situations and opportunities for our clients.

When the day finally came for our camp, it was a great success. Kids were learning and having fun, parents were beaming, and our athletes were happy to be having a positive impact in the community. We had handled all the details and logistics, allowing Wes and our other clients to show up and do what they were there for: teaching the kids about baseball. I may be biased, but I have to say they looked like heroes.

While our focus had been on planning Wes's involvement with the camp, I was also able to deepen our relationship to the point that he wanted to know more about me and our firm. After several more formal meetings and presentations, we signed Wes and we continue to represent him and his family today.

Do you think we would have signed Wes if I had simply sent him a page listing our qualifications as an agency? Do you think Leeman would have offered me my first job with the Super Bowl if I had only sent him a cover letter? Most important, do you still think it was luck that generated these opportunities?

Of course not! I didn't know Wes personally the day I first had a chance to work out with him. I didn't know Leeman as I entered the lobby of the Atlanta hotel where the ASC meeting was being held. Although I met them at two very different points in my career, I took the same attitude with both. Before I met either one, I already viewed each of them as someone who I could add value to and someone who was important for me to build a relationship with. I viewed both of them as people I wanted to buy into me—literally and figuratively. I just had to find a way to close the distance between us. I did, and good things came from it.

The Way the Job Market Really Works

I know the career you want is out there for you. And I know you probably don't have a relationship with the people who will hire you. Wouldn't it be great if you had a career agent working on your behalf when you were searching for this job? Someone who could engage people for you and get them excited about your passion and your vision for your career goals? Someone who would build a network of people that respect you?

Someone who would set up productive meetings with people in your industry and follow up for you afterwards? My role at Career Sports & Entertainment is to be the career agent for our clients. I will show you how to be your own career agent and be different from everybody else.

You *can* have this. You can be different from everybody else. You can be your own agent by closing the relationship gap.

Everybody else thinks the way to pursue a career is to conduct a mass-marketing campaign. Everybody else throws out a big net to see what they might catch. Everybody else scans job sites on the Web for opportunities. Everybody else blindly submits hundreds of resumes to hundreds of organizations, hoping one prospective employer somewhere will take notice. It can be very easy to fall in with the crowd of everybody else and believe that a mass-marketing campaign is the best route.

The people who choose to approach their careers like everybody else will probably end up being like everybody else. Like everybody else, they will move from interview to interview, trying to find a match. Like everybody else, they will encounter all the ways potential employers will test them (both directly and subtly) to discover what kinds of employees they might be. Like everybody else, their resumes will probably become lost in the hundreds of resumes in the filing cabinet of a Director of Human Resources. They are hoping that somehow, somewhere, somebody will find the real person inside of all that paper. They are hoping that lightning will strike, that magic will happen, that the impossible will come true. But in the end, they are just like everybody else.

Relationships Trump Resumes

Here is an important way to be different from everybody else:

> Accept that the way to pursue your career has less to do with resumes and more to do with relationships.

Every time I have an opportunity to talk to people who have successfully pursued their dream job, I have found that their game plan was based on strategies similar to my own. It's all about relationships, not resumes.

Resumes are one way of impressing a person, but they are not the only way (and not even the best way) to do this. Resumes are a platform to display your stats. There are fantastic books available on writing your resume and your cover letter. Pop into your college bookstore and browse around or visit JIST online at www.jist.com. Buy some books you think might be helpful in polishing your attempt to convey who you are on paper.

Similarly, the Internet is a wonderful resource for identifying jobs and for putting your name out among everybody else. Monster, CareerBuilder, Yahoo! HotJobs, and other Internet job boards do connect people with jobs. But which do you think would be better for you in the long run—having your resume on Monster along with millions of others, or having a person you know inside your target company helping you?

What I hope you see is that relationships trump resumes. And they trump them every time. The problem is that resumes are one dimensional, whereas relationships are multifaceted, dynamic, and personal. Relationships can lead to more people and new opportunities, but a resume can't introduce you to anyone new. Companies hire through relationships, not resumes. Why do I say this? Because organizations are made up of people. People read the resumes you send in. People make decisions about who to invite for interviews. And people make the hiring decisions after those interviews. Your resume is important, but it is the relationships you develop that will make the difference. So why wait to build these relationships?

The Relationship Gap

I know what you're thinking now. As you start your job search, you are thinking that you don't know anyone who has a job open in the big leagues of your field. And you are thinking that you don't know how many people you will have to connect with before you find an opportunity. You might be one person, or two people, or five people away from the person who will hire you. You're right: You don't know how far away from your dream job you really are. I call the distance between you and that job the *relationship gap*.

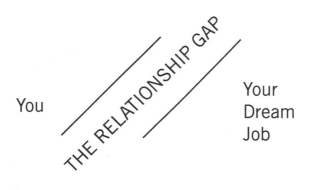

Figure 2.1: The Relationship Gap.

I am using the word "relationship" in a different way than you might use it to describe your best friend. Relationship in a job search means that you have spent enough energy and time learning to understand the world of the person you are meeting with, and have explained yourself enough that he or she understands your goals. A relationship means you have positioned and conducted yourself in a way that this person would be willing to help you by meeting with you again, introducing you to a colleague or associate, or possibly even connecting you with someone he or she respects who might or might not be hiring at his or her company.

This is what I mean when I say you must close the relationship gap: You have to learn to use and leverage the relationships you have in order to build more relationships. Remember, a key part of your job search strategy is building relationships with people who respect and like you enough to either help you or hire you. And there are very, very few resumes that—by themselves—will lead someone to want to help you.

Resumes and cover letters just don't do a good job of communicating what corporate psychologists call *key competencies*. The key competencies are the critical knowledge, skills, personality styles, and abilities needed to perform a particular job. You will convey your competencies in part through your experiences and in part through your style. Forming a relationship with someone who can see your passion, your skills, and your competencies can be invaluable.

My approach will make you focus on relationships, both with people you know and people you don't know (yet). Then, you must use these relationships to ask for advice. You will not be using your relationships to ask for a job, however; you will be using them to demonstrate who you are and what you are passionate about.

Wrapping Up and Moving On

Embrace the value of relationships in your job search.

CHAPTER 3

Five-Tool Players Make the Big Leagues

The secret to making the big leagues—in baseball, in golf, and in your career—is centered on a few simple ideas that can be incredibly hard to do:

Fearlessly executing your game plan with passionate style that will create career choices for yourself.

How do ball players get to the major leagues? They demonstrate to the people they want to play for—the people scouting them—that they have the tools they need and the ability to improve these tools.

In this chapter I'll give you an example of the tools you need and how one of our clients put these tools to use and made it to the major leagues. I'll also help you begin to identify the characteristics of your own necessary career tools.

Jeff Francoeur Creates Choices for Himself

When Jeff Francoeur (who became the Atlanta Braves' right fielder) was in high school, he demonstrated tremendous talent and athleticism on both the baseball and football fields. He was, and still is, a superior athlete. As a baseball player, then, he knew he could someday play at the major-league level. As a football player, he knew he could start for a Division I program and later pursue a professional career in the NFL. He put up big numbers and had choices as to whether he wanted to pursue a football or baseball career at a high level. It was no surprise that he was ranked by TeamOneBaseball.com and Rivals.com as the number-one two-sports prep athlete in the nation.

Because he had multiple tools, he created choices for himself. With this level of talent, Jeff had the attention of big-time college football programs as well as baseball scouts—including those from his hometown Major League Baseball team, the Atlanta Braves. These scouts saw him as a player who could hit for power as well as for average. He had an incredible throwing arm—what pros call a "cannon." He had good speed and his path to the ball would improve with more experience in game situations.

In early June 2002, Jeff was the 23rd overall pick by the Braves in the Major League Baseball draft. Now he had a chance to join a team he had looked up to all his life and play alongside a group of players, such as John Smoltz and Tom Glavine, whom he had idolized. Because his passion was baseball and his dream was to play at the Major League level, baseball was the route he went.

Scouting Talent

As the head of the Client Representation division, my job is not only managing our existing clients, but also procuring new clients. I have to sell athletes, coaches, and broadcasters on the capabilities of our firm—that's another way of saying that a big part of my job is focused on closing a relationship gap. Of course, we love when established, big-name stars sign on with us. But we also try to form relationships with players who are earlier in their careers—those who are still coming up—and work with them to help them manage their choices and develop to their full potentials.

When agents, scouts, and Major League Baseball front-office personnel look for talented baseball players, they have to predict how a player might perform in the big leagues. They might have data from high school stats or college ball, but there is no surefire way to predict how a player will perform in the big leagues. Pick any major sport—baseball, football, basketball, hockey—and I can tell you a story of a phenomenal kid who just couldn't make the transition to the professional level. Having great stats in the past is important, but these stats just don't guarantee success in the future.

So agents, scouts, and general managers evaluate a young baseball player not only on his amateur performance, but also on his *potential* to continue to do well in professional ball. Because they can't know for certain how a player will do in the big leagues, they look for predictors of performance. Talk to any MLB general manager and he (or one day more "she"s) will tell you there are five major indicators:

- Hitting for power

- Hitting for average

- Fielding ability

- Speed

- Throwing ability

The best, most desirable players are strong in all these categories, and are described as "five-tool" players. A five-tool player will make the big leagues because he has the potential to contribute in many different ways: at the plate—with power and consistency; and in the field—with speed, great defense, and a strong arm.

Think of the baseball GM and the team manager as equivalent to the hiring manager for your dream job. Employers are looking for talent, too. But just like a rookie coming out of school, you haven't proven yourself yet. You might have a resume that has important information (your stats from the past), but these are not a perfect indicator of how you will do on the job. So employers scout your *potential and coachability.*

A hiring manager knows that there is much you still have to learn, so she looks at your fundamentals. She is trying to decide whether all the tools for success are present or attainable.

In the most desirable jobs, the competition is tough, so employers look for employees who are strong in multiple areas. Just like a baseball player, you have the best chance of getting the job if you have multiple strengths. You don't have to hit for power or average and so on, but you must become a five-tool player of a different sort.

The Five Tools for Your Career Success

Many qualities will be important to you in becoming your own career agent, but these are the five most important tools of your search process. To make the big leagues, you must develop and demonstrate the following tools.

Tool 1: Your Passionate Style

It all starts with passion. Before you can think about playing in the big leagues, you have to have the energy and drive to withstand the rigors of getting there, and passion is what must drive you. Passion is what immediately separates those who will *make it happen* from those who *hope it happens,* because passion is about having belief in your vision and the willingness to persevere in critical times.

Here are just a few examples of what passion is:

- Passion is what inspires a pitcher to rehab for months after surgery because of the desire to get back on the field.

- Passion is what motivates a coach to focus on his recruiting strategy for the following season just 12 hours after winning a national championship.

- Passion is what motivates a 20th-round MLB draft pick to accept a signing bonus of just $1,000 and three years of minor-league baseball just to stay in pursuit of his dream. Day after day and year after year, he will continue to step on a bus for another 12-hour road trip, all in hopes of proving himself—and improving his tools—to get to the big leagues.

- Passion is what fuels a professional golfer schlepping across the country paying entry fees, finding the cheapest hotels, and having his girlfriend or wife be his caddie to save a couple bucks because one day he believes he will win and make it all worthwhile.

These are true stories from people I've met and managed in my career. It was their passion—pure and simple—that energized them and kept them going through the difficult times as they closed the gap between their current situation and their dream. Passion is what must energize you, too. It's what will wake you up when you are exhausted and will keep you focused on your vision. Your style is the way in which you will express your passion. It is the tone and pace of your speech. It is each and every nonverbal signal you send during your interviews. When you successfully combine passion and style, you will bring your skills, personal qualities, and potential to life for others to see.

Chapters 4 and 5 are about developing and using your own passionate style.

Tool 2: Your Fearlessness

Evander Holyfield, the world-famous boxer, has a passion for boxing, but he also has the fearlessness to step into the ring fight after fight. He has the fearlessness to crawl back to his feet after a right hook from Mike Tyson.

Jeff Francoeur is passionate about the game of baseball, but it is his fearlessness that allows him to step back into the batter's box days after being hit in the face with a 95 mph fastball.

Both a young person looking for that perfect job and an athlete looking to put up good numbers needs fearlessness to recover from adversity. In some ways, you have it easy. Your challenges are less likely to be physical and more likely to be emotional. You will be drained at times and you will get frustrated, but it's pretty unlikely you will take a punch from Tyson or have a fastball thrown right under your chin during the course of your job search!

Fearlessness is the way your passion is brought to life in your behavior. It is unbeatable persistence. It is confidence and belief in yourself. It is your ability to embrace challenges without allowing the fear of failure to inhibit your efforts. It is your guts and your tenacity.

Having fear or worry is not the issue. Everyone does at one time or another. But you must control it before it controls you. How do you control fear? Fear can be overcome by successful experiences and great preparation. You can use your passion to send positive messages and positive visuals to yourself, such as "I'm going to nail this interview" or "I can't wait to get into this field." Fearlessness helps you overcome the negative thoughts that may creep in, such as "They were right: This is impossible" or "I guess I'm just not good enough." You must believe in your dream enough to not allow the "no" messages to stand in your way. One of the biggest differences between good and great is someone's ability to recover from adversity—and to do so quickly. You must have fearlessness to recover and embrace life's forthcoming and unexpected challenges with vigor. This fearlessness is one of the primary ingredients for landing your dream career. Chapters 6 and 7 help you cultivate your own fearlessness.

Tool 3: Your Game Plan

Your game plan will be your road map. It will become your tangible, step-by-step guide to pursuing your dream job.

We represent some pretty inspirational guys as clients. In a pre-game locker-room speech, one of our basketball coaches might pump up his players by telling them, "Our five guys are better than their five guys…this is our game to win, so play to win, don't play not to lose." At halftime, I've seen one of my coaches give speeches filled with awesome vigor and intensity.

I've seen our coaches rally their teams to come-from-behind wins. But their passion isn't the whole picture. Our coaches have a game plan as well. They have a plan for defending the opponent's star player. They know the x's and o's of winning a basketball game.

Each of our big-league pitchers spends hours studying the batting habits of the team he will face. Then he creates a plan for how he is going to pitch each hitter: down and away for one, off-speed pitches for another, and so on. Some of our other clients spend the same amount of time studying *him* so that they know how to hit him. They try to know his best pitches, his movement on the ball, his setup pitches, and his out pitches. They also have a plan of attack so that they can anticipate the best opportunities to connect.

You, too, must pinpoint your path for successfully executing and securing your dream career. Your game plan allows you to anticipate opportunities and challenges. You must create the tangible and intangible resources to put yourself in the best possible position. A successful game plan has proper and thorough preparation for your audiences. It involves time and research. It requires tremendous preparation in order to handle the curve balls you will see coming from someone who is equally prepared.

Chapters 8 through 10 deal with how to formulate your own career game plan.

Tool 4: Your Flawless Execution

No matter how passionate a speech Michigan State University Head Men's Basketball Coach Tom Izzo gives in the locker room and no matter how carefully he has crafted his game plan, when the ball goes up in the air at tipoff, his players must execute. When one of our golfers puts his ball on the tee at the #1 hole at the AT&T Tour event on a warm Thursday in May, his livelihood will ride on his ability to execute. When one of our pitchers steps on the mound or one of our position players steps into the box—whether it's April or October—it's show time. When the Fresnel lights come up on one of our broadcasters in the booth, she must deliver her script and her message flawlessly.

Making it all real and bringing it to life in the moment is imperative to being successful. This is why execution is one of the most important of the five tools. Flawless execution is demonstrating your passionate style and your fearlessness and bringing to life your game plan within your interactions. Execution is your ability to appropriately conduct yourself in your phone calls and your meetings. Execution is carefully choosing the words you put into the e-mails you send.

As you execute your game plan, you will find yourself in front of people you know and people you don't know. You will be securing opportunities to "wow" people in formal interviews and informational interviews. If you can't or don't deliver in the moment, you will ride the bench! Execution is the glue that will pull together your passion, your fearlessness, and your game plan and bring them to life. Execution is what makes it all real.

Chapters 11 through 14 are about executing the various phases of your job search.

Tool 5: Your Great Management of Choices

If you have been a four-tool player up to now, you will be a five-tool player going forward. Your execution—which requires passion, fearlessness, and a game plan—will create choices. Your passion, your fearlessness, your game plan, and your execution are opening doors and you are choosing which ones to walk through. Choices are a product of hard work, of executing against your plan, and of making opportunities a reality. You are in control of your life when you create choices for yourself and that will make you happier. How you manage these choices—your fifth tool— is critical.

Haven't you ever been in a situation where you felt a lack of control? And wasn't it a paralyzing feeling? Think of a home run leader who is now free agent: He has new choices. Think of a successful and talented football coach who has just taken his team to the BCS title: He has new alternatives. Think of an LPGA player who has lead the tour just as her endorsement deals are concluding: She has options.

At the most basic, self-fulfilling level, you are working to be wanted and to create leverage for yourself. Chapters 15 and 16 are about creating choices for yourself and managing them effectively.

Putting It All Together

Are you a five-tool player today? Can you identify which tools you feel good about and which ones you need to strengthen? You must be able to because these five tools are the foundation of a truly successful job search and career.

Take an honest look at yourself. Maybe you think you already apply three or four of the tools effectively and that is enough. Or maybe you really do understand the basic blueprint for success, but don't understand how the *process* works. But if you think the best strategy is to send out hundreds of resumes and hope things will fall into place, put this book down.

If you are still reading, you have successfully adjusted your thinking relevant to the job search process. You realize that *all five tools are important.* Just like in baseball, being outstanding in two of the five will not get you to the big leagues as an everyday player. You need to be strong in all the tools. Two or three of these tools will probably come naturally to you, but you will have to work to improve on the others. Improving the weaker tools is often the hardest part, but it's worth the effort.

To pursue your dream career, you will have to practice new skills and think about things in a way that you don't normally do. Rising to this challenge is one of the first things that will help you stand out. Rising to the challenge of improving your weaker tools will bring out your passion for life and its opportunities. So don't be like everybody else. Become a five-tool player and get to the big leagues—and stay there!

Wrapping Up and Moving On

All five tools are important. In the next part of the book, you will learn about the first tool: your passionate style.

Tool One: Your Passionate Style

CHAPTER 4

Passion and Style

I had most of the five tools when I sat in Lonnie's office. I was passionate, I was fearless, and I was executing my game plan. What I still wanted and needed were choices. This meant I had to look inside myself to honestly answer his questions: "Who are you? And what do you want to do?" On the surface, I could have answered them literally, by telling him about my background and where I saw my career going. But Lonnie's real question to me was about my passion: "What do you know about yourself that you will bring into your career?"

Most people you will talk to in your career quest—be they informational contacts or formal interviewers—will ask you a similar question. Before you can answer it, you must know your own passion and you must be able to demonstrate it.

What Is Passion?

To play in the big leagues of your chosen career, you must be passionate about what you're doing. Passion is the heart of commitment; it is your center and your core. Although passion is intangible, it is arguably what defines you because it energizes you and gives you a sense of urgency. Passion is the outward expression of how important something or someone really is to you.

Passion is also a key part of being consistently, uniquely, and respectfully persistent. When you have a passion for your potential career, the process of finding your job can be a natural part of each and every day.

When our athletes talk about their passion, they say that it's what drives them to play through the pain. The best athletes play with passion (and have a sense of urgency) because they know their business is competitive and that there is always someone right behind them ready to take their job. And, subconsciously, they know they have a limited window of time to use their bodies to make the money that must last them a lifetime.

You have a window of time, also, and—whether you know it or not—there is someone else competing to take your dream job. So allow your passion to overwhelm you and motivate you. You are looking for the tough jobs and so is everybody else. Your passion and your sense of urgency are how you will make it to the big leagues.

A Passion for the Game

One of our clients, Tom Izzo, the coach of the Michigan State University men's basketball team, illustrates passion. In April 2000, the team finished a successful regular Big Ten season and headed off to March Madness. As they beat Valparaiso, Utah, Syracuse, and Iowa State to advance to the Final Four, I could see Tom becoming more and more immersed in the opportunity to lock up a national championship. His passion for the game was demonstrated by his focus and his drive. By the Wisconsin game, Tom was intently focused on getting past a team that had already beaten them once in the regular season and was again a barrier to his goal. Tom's passion was transferred and injected into his players and led to his team's successful on-court execution.

In the final with Florida, Tom was knocking on the door of his first national championship. But his passion didn't begin or end with his pre-game locker room or his half-time speeches. It was a part of every minute, every possession, and every on-court decision. That's what it takes to win national championships—not just from the coach, but from the players as well. Tom's passion became the pulse of his players, too. The rest is history, as the team took home the championship.

Tom's passion didn't end with this victory. His love for the game was deeper than that. At midnight on a Monday night, Tom was celebrating a national championship, hoisted on the shoulders of his players, and making the final cut to bring down the net. But Tuesday morning, instead of relaxing and taking a moment for himself, Tom was on the phone with his coaches, discussing their recruiting game plan. That's passion.

Tom's passion for the team doesn't extend to just the players on the court; it's for all of those who made the championship possible. As intense as he can be walking the bench, he is a very unselfish, team-oriented, and university-minded guy. He even gave the janitor at the Breslin Center a championship ring.

What's Your Passion?

Passion is what will sustain your motivation to take the extra steps needed to be different from everybody else and overcome roadblocks and barriers. So what is your passion? Ask yourself questions such as the following:

- What do you do when you have free time?

- What causes you to lose track of time?

- When you walk into a bookstore, what section do you head toward?

- When you have nothing you have to think about, what do you think about?

- What would people who know you describe as your greatest strengths?

Search for your passion, because it will become your foundation. I can't tell you what your passion is, but I know you have something somewhere inside you that creates it. You'll know it when you find it. And you can learn to channel it and utilize it.

When I packed up my Honda Accord and headed south to Atlanta— without a job—I had passion. I had a feel for sports marketing and what I believed to be some of my strengths. I still didn't know that I wanted to be a sports agent, but I knew I wanted to work in the business of sports. I wasn't afraid to admit that I didn't know exactly what I wanted to do. I knew that the more great people I could get in front of, the more I would learn how to match up my strengths with a unique opportunity.

When people share with you what they do and how they do it, you gain knowledge. You also better discover what excites you. When you find yourself getting excited about their worlds, you've begun to bring out the passion inside of you and to better understand yourself.

Displaying Passion Through Your Style

It was my passion that led me to end up in Lonnie's office. And how I displayed my passion was through my style. Lonnie sensed my sincerity and knew that my interest was in the business side of sports—he knew I wasn't a fan. My energy was apparent but controlled as I sat on the edge of the chair in his office and shared my interests. He later told me that the style I displayed in his office in our first meeting was the style he felt matched up to working with the clients.

What Exactly Is Style?

Most young people understand style, even if they can't easily define it. Style is the collection of intangibles that people demonstrate at various moments when they're communicating with others. Style is the way people capitalize on moments and use them for the betterment of the relationship. Style is, at the most basic level, the method and approach you make relevant to your communication. For your friends, your style is a reflection of your interests, your values, your beliefs, and other qualities that make you interesting. For an employer, your style is a reflection on your drive, your motivations, and how you are likely to behave on the job.

What Kind of Style Is Impressive to Potential Employers?

Because your style is a form of communication, you must be attentive to both the nonverbal and the verbal elements of every interaction: your tone of voice, the pace of the conversation and your eye contact. Additionally, be attentive to your surroundings.

Your tone needs to display an individual who is confident but not cocky. It shouldn't be a whisper, but certainly it shouldn't be loud enough for someone in an office next door to hear the conversation. Take on a somewhat speedy but deliberate pace. That sends a message relevant to your respect for your contact's time and your inherent sense of urgency. Eye contact is imperative. You might look away briefly, but certainly ensure that when you are answering questions and when he is speaking to you, you are locked in on him. Additionally, recognize and comment on a picture in his office or something that he seems obviously proud of. Congratulate him or simply show sincere interest.

Style isn't just being attentive; it's also knowing how and when to respond. An impressive style is an intangible, but we all know it when we see it. People with an impressive style are impressive because they handle every issue through the eyes of the other person. They adapt their styles to the needs of others and the things happening at that moment. They are flexible and have what psychologists like Daniel Goleman call *emotional intelligence*. Goleman says there are four skills to master (and while we are all born with different natural levels of each skill, all can be practiced and learned):

- **Self-awareness:** Understanding your own emotions and motivations, as well as how they influence your behavior. When you are having an interview or an advice meeting, you need to be very aware of your emotions. Don't label every feeling as "nerves" or "worry." Figure out exactly what you are feeling.

- **Self-management:** Controlling the impact your emotions have on your behavior. If you know exactly what you are feeling, you can work to control how you are expressing that feeling. Is your nervousness making you think more about what you want to say than about really listening to the person you are talking to? Are you so excited and happy about what you are hearing that you are losing your professional demeanor? Are you so afraid you will be rejected that you are giving up too early and not asking the insightful questions that would show your passion?

- **Social awareness:** Being able to see and understand the emotions and motivations of others. You need to accurately "decode" the communications coming your way. Is the interviewer tense? Maybe you should say, "I really appreciate this time, knowing how busy you are. I think we can do this very quickly." Is the interviewer starting to look bored? Maybe you should speed up or move on to another topic. Is the interviewer becoming frustrated? Maybe you should make sure you are listening as much as you are talking.

- **Relationship management:** Putting together these skills to connect, bond, and influence others. Your meeting—interview or advice—is the first opportunity to begin to build a relationship. You will continue to build the relationship with your actions after you leave by how you follow up and take the next steps.

As you can see, having emotional intelligence allows you to adapt yourself to the situation at hand (that is, the style of person interviewing you) but still remain in control of the messages you communicate through your style. Being flexible and responding to the situation at hand doesn't mean you are not being real. Instead, it means that you can draw on the many different strengths you possess and choose the one that is most appropriate for the situation. For example, when I'm in front of client like John Smoltz (longtime Atlanta Braves pitcher and Cy Young winner) and when I am in front of my mom, I demonstrate two different styles.

With John, I am a professional, a negotiator, an ambassador, and a businesswoman. But I must also weave through my communications that I can be someone he not only respects, but also enjoys. I'm always "on"; I'm always anticipating, reading, and responding. Because he's the client and I'm not, I have to be very attuned to his interests. He's the guy who gets to decide how far to push the needle in a negotiation; we can make our recommendations and provide stats to support them. But in the end, it is his life and his contract, so the buck stops with him. My job is to make sure the relationship has been built on mutual respect so that our experience and advice are heard.

With my mom, I am her daughter. I can talk without anticipating, without perfect preparation and knowledge of her yesterdays and her tomorrows. There are few people in life that you can be transparent with as your life and career progress. Often in relationships anchored with unconditional love, you don't have to attend to your style as much.

Remember, people hire people. First they look for respectable stats. Then they look for intangibles such as great style, which reflects your strong passion.

Wrapping Up and Moving On

Passion and style are the fuel in the engine of your job search. Next you'll see how to reveal them in all your interactions with potential employers and informational contacts.

CHAPTER 5

Sell Yourself, Not Your Resume

Passion and style are important because the relationship gap between you and your dream job is real and these tools help close it. There are more applicants for great jobs than there are great job openings. So you must use these tools (along with the others in this book) to differentiate yourself from the other candidates.

My own career started with challenges. I sat in front of plenty of executives who told me, "You can't break into sports marketing; it's just too competitive" or, "You never played professionally" or even, "You're a woman." No one came to me as a student at Michigan State and asked me to please, please, pretty please come work for me in sports marketing. The business is very competitive. There is simply not enough room for all the people who would like to be in the big leagues of the business of sports.

Sending my resume to people I didn't know would have gotten me nowhere. This chapter is about how to break out of the traditional resume-driven job search and show your true self—and the intangibles that set you apart from the crowd—to potential employers.

Following the "Rules" Will Not Get You Hired

Many young people I see make the mistake of trying to sell their credentials—their school, their grades, or their experiences. This is understandable. You've been told to focus on marketing *your story*, as opposed to marketing *who you are through your passion and style*. I see young adults casting out a large net—sending resumes and cover letters nearly randomly in response to job postings and going to career fairs alongside everyone else—but having no idea what they will catch, if they will like it, and whether it will be the start of their dream career. They have very little way of knowing whether the job they might secure really matches up with who they are and their skills.

With this prevalent mindset, it's no surprise that there is a huge market for books and resources on finding a job. But many of these really aren't good "how-to" guides. Often these other resources start by asking you to believe that finding a job is a matter of mass-marketing yourself. Send out lots and lots of creative letters and resumes and wait for job opportunities to come to you. So many of the books, articles, and Web sites out there still push these ideas, even though they are hopelessly out-of-date and passive.

All of your life, you have been encouraged to work hard but "follow the rules." You've been told what homework to do, and you've done it. You were told which classes to take for your major, and you took them. Whether or not you see it, you have learned to live like you were inside a box. You've learned the boundaries, and you believe that if you stay within them, success will find you.

Think back on those classes. Like most people who want to succeed, you probably quickly learned to size up the amount of work you would have to do to earn the minimum grade you wanted. So when it came time to take the first steps on the way to your career, you probably started searching for the "rules" to finding a job. You probably believed that by playing by the rules of the game, you would be rewarded with the job of your dreams.

The main problem with the conventional wisdom on job searching is that you are being taught to do the things that are least likely to get you hired. Why? Because as I've said before, your resume isn't going to get you hired. You have to understand that the real way that organizations hire people does not line up with the way you have been taught to look for a job. The truth is, when you just e-mail, fax, or send your resume to someone you don't know, you can expect that 99.99 percent of the time you will not get that job. If you get a response at all, it will be something like the following:

Dear Ms. Carruthers:

Thank you for your interest in Dream Careers, Inc.

It appears from your resume that you have gained experience that will be very beneficial in your job search. Unfortunately, we have no positions available that match your qualifications.

We will keep your resume on file for one year in the event that a position for which you are qualified arises.

Again, we thank you for your interest in Dream Careers, Inc. Good luck in all your future endeavors.

Sincerely,

Steve Kincaid

A Personal Approach Works Better

Over the years, I've closely watched students who are looking for jobs, especially jobs with Career Sports & Entertainment. I've read their cover letters and reviewed their resumes. I've seen approaches that work and approaches that, more often than not, don't. From my own experience watching these applicants, I've come to realize that while just sending out resumes isn't the way to get that dream job, there is a formula that works. It's a different approach, a formula built around personal relationships—around understanding how to close the relationship gap.

The Process of Getting Known

Cover letters and resumes are not the solution to your challenge. They are important, but they do not, by themselves, land the dream jobs. They are not the primary reason companies hire the people they do.

When organizations line up candidates from the outside (that is, not promoting someone from within the organization), they use the following order of priority:

1.   Referrals from trusted peers

2.   Candidates supplied by career fairs, recruitment drives, search firms, or employment agencies

3.   Responses to want ads and Web sites

4.   Unsolicited resumes

If you look, there is a clear pattern here: The more the organization knows you as a person, the more likely they are to consider you a legitimate candidate. They look first to those they have relationships with and to those they know. This is absolutely true for senior-level positions, but it shouldn't be a surprise that it's also true for entry-level jobs. Research conducted by Watson Wyatt (a worldwide human resources consulting firm) found that companies that hire based on referrals are more financially successful and that the people they hire are more dedicated and committed on the job.

Social psychologists know that it takes repeated contact with a new person before you can feel you know, understand, and trust them. And there is no reason for an organization to trust a piece of paper (your resume). Why should they? Research has shown that up to a third of all applicants lie in some way on their resume—even head coach George O'Leary, who had to resign from the University of Notre Dame's football program after it came to light that he had inaccurately reported on his resume certain key details of his educational background.

This means the human resources department will be much more helpful to you after you are hired than before. Before you are hired, they will serve as a screening agency or a barrier you must get past. Clearly, you will be better off if you can meet someone in person instead of relying on your resume to do the talking for you.

Zig Zigler, the sales and motivational guru, says the first time you meet someone, they feel you are a stranger. The second time, they feel you are vaguely familiar. The third time, they feel you are an acquaintance. The fourth time, they feel they know you. Why would you expect it be any different in the workplace? Once you understand this, it should be clear that your primary focus should be not on tweaking your resume but on making personal connections with the people who can help you. To do so, you must separate yourself from everybody else. You must understand the most effective ways to show your strengths and your attractiveness as an employee. You must be your own career agent. But as you'll see in the next section, the direct route is usually not the best route.

Don't Be Too Direct

Even if the best looking, nicest, funniest, and richest guy in the world asked me to marry him within the first 15 minutes of meeting me, I'd think he was arrogant, rude, and inappropriate. It's no different in your career search. In fact, in many ways, your career search *is* like dating. You have to know "how to date"—that is, you have to have the ability and the willingness to spend the time and energy needed to build relationships—to be successful in either your job search or your dating search. Author Shawn Graham expands this idea into a complete book in *Courting Your Career* (www.courtingyourcareer.com).

In the movie *The Godfather,* Michael Corleone must hide in 1940s Sicily after committing a crime in the United States (but that's not the point of this story). While in Sicily, walking through the outskirts of town, he passes a beautiful woman and is immediately struck by her beauty. Michael speaks limited Sicilian, so he must rely on his guards as they go into town to try to locate this beautiful woman again.

Stopping at a restaurant, one of the guards asks the owner, "Do you know all the girls around here? We saw some real beauties. One of them struck our friend like a thunderbolt. She would tempt the devil himself. Really put together...such hair! ...such a mouth! This one had a purple dress, and a purple ribbon in her hair, more Greek than Italian. Do you know her?"

Suddenly, the restaurant owner stands up angrily and says, "No! There's no girl like that in this town!" He spins around and walks away.

The guard quickly realizes the woman must be the restaurant owner's daughter, and that he insulted the owner with his crude description of his daughter's beauty. So he tries to hurry Michael away before the father returns and real trouble breaks out. Michael also realizes that the guards have violated some social norm of the culture, but insists on speaking to the father himself, with the guard translating.

"I apologize if we offended you," he tells the father in a respectful but persistent manner. "I am a stranger in this country and I meant no disrespect to you or your daughter. I want to meet your daughter with your permission and under the supervision of your family, with all respect."

Wow, the father thinks, perhaps there is something more here in this young man than I first saw. With this approach, the father calms down and invites Michael to dinner to meet his daughter, Apollonia. Over the course of the next few weeks, Michael and Apollonia eat dinner together, always in the presence of her family. They take long walks through town, closely chaperoned by her sisters and aunts. And after a period of time, Michael marries Apollonia with the full blessing of her father.

To pull the analogy back full circle for you, Michael first presented his "cover letter" through the guard (who didn't do it very well). Michael decided to be his own agent. He was initially misunderstood, but through his persistent and respectful style, he was able to better present himself to the father and earn the chance to be introduced to Apollonia. A piece of paper is just one-dimensional and demonstrates no style, but when you create dialogue—as Michael did—you demonstrate your style and create new opportunities.

Intangibles and Tangibles

You can distinguish yourself through your *intangibles*. The intangibles are what help you stand out from the crowd and show your passionate style. You probably have not had enough professional work experiences in your dream career yet to point to as a tangible indicator of your potential. This means that any intangibles you can convey are important during your first real job search in your dream field. You must show that you have the necessary tools and qualities to be successful, even if you haven't had a chance to practice them yet.

Let's clarify what we mean by tangibles and intangibles. Many of the other books on finding a job basically tell you that it is just a mechanical process. Everybody else will try to convince you that finding the start of your career is like working a machine: pull this lever, twist that knob, and push that button and wait for a great job to pop out.

The levers, knobs, and buttons that everybody else seems to focus on are the *tangibles*. The tangibles are really nothing more than the qualifiers and credentials needed to get you into the game. They don't help you win. They show employers that you can put forth the necessary effort, but they won't be enough by themselves to create your dream career. Tangibles only provide opportunities to learn about you without ever meeting you personally. As a result, tangibles play only a small role in the final (and most critical) decisions of any hiring process. Intangibles, however, are critical.

Can Your Resume Actually Hurt You?

Frankly, when you don't have a lot of experience in your dream career, resumes can hurt you more than they can help you. Very few young people coming out of college have ever been offered a unique or great job based on their resume alone. And many people looking to switch to a dream career have lost opportunities because of their resumes. Very few students have earned a job offer based on a clever cover letter alone. Many more have had a poor cover letter cause them to be relegated to the "do not hire" pile. Now, don't misunderstand me: Resumes do matter and are important, but they are not what will win you a job at this point in your life. Your resume is just a brochure, but you are the product that must be purchased.

A young person's resume is likely to consist of educational background, summer jobs, and perhaps a professional internship he or she has secured if they were proactive. And if you are changing careers, your resume is full of experience that might not be easily or noticeably applicable to your dream career. But college GPAs and past employment really only serve as a first level of screening for potential employers; they are an indication that you worked hard, learned, and were successful in the more significant challenges so far in your life.

Your grades and your resume are very important predictors (and maybe the only predictors you have so far in your career), but they are not *perfect* predictors for whether you will be successful on this job. Yes, having a degree from the right school or great management experience in other fields can help you open some doors, but you can't expect that these will close any deals on their own. In fact, after you secure your first job in your dream career, your degree and much of your past experience rarely matter again, but your intangibles live on. Having your degree and proving you can succeed in school or on a job are the ticket to get you into the ballpark, but they don't guarantee you'll hit any home runs.

The next time you are with friends who are getting ready to start careers, take a quick look at where they are putting their energies. Are they focusing only on tangibles? Are they eagerly writing resumes, touching up cover letters, and browsing job sites on the Web to find out where they can send their clever cover letters and resumes? Are they all taking the same approach to starting their careers? Do you see anything they are doing that will help them stand out from everybody else? And even if they are doing something different, do they believe that simply writing a *better* resume and cover letter will make them stand out?

The Importance of Bringing Out the Intangibles

Although you have to have the skills needed for the job you are seeking, you must also have the intangible personal qualities that employers find appealing. Do you know what employers are looking for when they make a hiring decision? Most research shows that the most important personal qualities employers seek are these:

- Communication skills

- Honesty

- The ability to work as part of a team

- A strong work ethic

- Strong analytical skills

These intangibles are very hard to convey in a letter or resume, but they are much more important than anything that is in your resume and cover letter. The intangibles—those things you say and do that tell who you are as a person in a way that a resume and cover letter just can't—have the biggest impact on the impression you will make, and are almost always what win you the job over other qualified candidates. It is the intangibles that put you over the top. The skills, drive, and passion you display in your search process will demonstrate that you "get it."

Because you probably do not have a great deal of real-life experience to show, your challenge when starting out in securing your dream career is making yourself stand out in ways that show you have the skills and the drive for the *specific kind of work* you want to do. The data used to make an initial impression about you will be based on your intangible qualities, not your work history. In many cases, your initial meeting with a potential employer might become a chance for them to "test-drive" you as a potential employee. You might not have a 10-year history of success, but you can show them you have the drive to start to build your history. You might not have a huge sales win to discuss, but you can show you have the interpersonal skills needed to be successful in sales. Intangibles are not only what will set you apart in meetings and interviews, but also what will help you show you have the competencies you need to be successful in the job you want.

Even though the process can seem overwhelming, remember that life isn't a warm-up. You have to pursue your dreams *now.* If you want to be like everybody else, go after your dream job by sending out resumes and cover letters and then waiting. But if you want to be different, if you want to wake up every day excited about the rest of your career, start showing your intangibles now. The next section shows you how.

Reveal Your Intangibles

Now that I've established how important the intangibles are, let's talk about how you can make them known. Here's an example of how our agency did just that with a prospective client.

Wowing Mark DeRosa with the Intangibles

Mark DeRosa is a professional baseball player. In the late 1990s, Mark was a highly touted prospect, a middle infielder, in the minor leagues of the Atlanta Braves organization. Mark had signed with another agent and firm when he came out of college, but in light of his relationship with our other clients, I was able to meet Mark and his wife, Heidi, on multiple occasions when he was in the minor leagues. They became acquaintances, and when I visited other clients, I would often see Mark. We would always say hello, and on some occasions he would go with me and our client to dinner.

So Mark had a general understanding of our firm and what we were about, but I kept my eye out for the appropriate time to create a more formal opportunity to familiarize Mark with our agency. My goal wasn't necessarily to immediately sign him, at least not yet. My goal was to raise Mark's awareness and interest in our firm, and gain his respect for what we do. He wasn't ready for us to ask him to "get married." We needed to date.

I arranged for him to have an interview with a local magazine, an interview I knew he would be interested in doing. Of course, I set up the meeting for this interview in our office. When he arrived, I quietly tried to wow him without being obvious. For example, I put the magazine writer in a conference room at the farthest corner of our floor to make sure Mark walked from one end of our office to the other. Before Mark arrived, I talked to people who knew him to learn more about his interests off the field.

When Mark arrived, I made sure he walked through all the divisions of our company. He got a taste of what we are all about by seeing the visuals on the walls of our client representation division, our media division, our events division, our corporate marketing division, our creative division, and our various other services. I made sure he walked by almost 100 sharp, energetic, and personable people who popped out of their offices and cubes to welcome him. As we walked, he mentioned several times, "I had no idea you guys were this big and did all this." And when we arrived in the back conference room for our meeting, I had three huge bowls of peanut M&Ms, which I had learned are his favorite candy, sitting on the table. I also had a signed Tom Brady jersey for him, which I knew he wanted to add to his memorabilia collection (something I had learned from those who knew him).

Needless to say, Mark was ready to hear about our professional abilities, too, and we wowed him. He had known about our agency because of our other baseball clients, but did not know our entire agency's capabilities, nor did he know us in our environment.

Over the next several weeks and months, I continued to show him glimpses of our skills and abilities. We were "dating." I continued to create more opportunities to show him the intangible reasons we were right for him. The one-hour experience he had in our office positioned us to earn the level of respect we needed so that, at the right time, we could ask for the opportunity to present our full services to him. And months later, after more formal and specific meetings, we signed him.

In my work, the intangible side is where I feel I add the most value—and is where I feel the most passionate. It's the conversation with a baseball player five minutes after he has learned he's been traded, reassuring him and his wife, and helping him embrace change. It's coaching a college coach to understand how to connect with his athletic director. It's helping the professional golfer understand the challenges of her first year on the Tour. And yes, it is exceeding their expectations whenever possible by negotiating lucrative contracts to maximize the window of time they have in their careers. And for our clients, that's a very important part of our work. But my passion is for procuring and managing the relationships our clients need.

How You Can Wow Your Contacts

As you start down the road of your dream career, you must realize that you are selling something intangible: yourself. Every time you interact with other people, you are communicating and being evaluated on multiple levels simultaneously. When you meet with your contacts, they will evaluate much more than what you say. They will evaluate your style, too.

Good marketers and salespeople actually have something they call the "wow factor." The wow factor is your ability to indirectly convey your passion, game plan, intellect, work ethic, skills, style, or other intangible qualities in a way that shows you are unique and valuable. You might impart the wow factor through a quality that you have, a story you share, the work that you have done, or the effort that you have made—but it is something that will impress this specific person at this specific moment, creating a reaction of "wow—that's something I wouldn't have expected—and it's special."

Creating wow moments are what will set you apart. How you prepare and build toward this moment in a business setting really isn't mysterious. There are two basic things you have to do. First, you need to research your contact and the company. Second, you need to learn something unique about the company and be able to demonstrate that knowledge in your meeting.

Do Your Research

First, you must do some preliminary research to educate yourself enough to understand your informational contact person or interviewer better on a personal and professional level. Just like I learned DeRosa liked M&Ms and wanted a Tom Brady jersey, you must research the people you are meeting with. This is the process, in many ways, of creating the "statistics" of your game plan.

On the personal level, create and then answer a list of questions, the answers to which will make you feel that you "know" the person you are going to meet. For example:

- Where is he from?

- Where did she attend college?

- Is he married?

- How long has she been with the company?

- Does he have children?

The Web is your fastest source of information on a company. Besides the official Web site, Yahoo! maintains summaries of all public companies and many large private companies; these are excellent resources for collecting information on the organizational history of a company and its performance. You can find a list of officers at every public company. You might want to do another search with their names to learn their interests, activities, and charitable causes. Although this is personal information, most high-level executives have some type of biography on their company's Web site.

Gathering information on people who aren't on a company's Web site or don't have a biography on their site can be more difficult but isn't impossible. Simply Google their name and be resourceful by finding the latest and greatest online resource to gather their information. More information isn't necessarily better. It's just important to try to uncover something that you don't think another person would have uncovered. (Maybe it's as elementary as finding out it's their birthday next week and asking them their birthday plans.)

If a Google search doesn't turn up anything, try going to the Web site of your local business newspaper (most cities have a weekly business newspaper) and search their site for the company name; although you might or might not find personal information on your contact, you will at least be as up-to-date as possible on the company.

When you find information on the person and the company, read it, learn it, remember it, and use it.

Collect any information you can on the company as well. On the professional level, there are many ways to find information on the company you are interested in, but the easiest is the Web. Spend at least an hour studying the company's Web site:

- Learn its mission and philosophy of business.

- Learn its business strategy and attempt to understand it enough to discuss it intelligently at the top-line level.

- Know the company's key clients.

- Study what the business does so that you can go into the meeting knowing how they make money. You would be amazed at how many people apply for jobs without really understanding this—the simplest metric of business.

You can also Google companies to find news stories and press releases that will help you understand recent events and issues. Go to the library and read recent magazine and newspaper articles on the organization; do the same thing for the organization's main competitors. Get copies of sales brochures and find customer reviews. For public companies, you can order and read their most recent annual report—one of the best ways to learn about an organization (you can usually find these on the company's Web site under the Investor Relations section). You can use this information to create a "wow" moment in your meetings.

Do not go into your first meeting until you can answer the following questions from memory:

- **What is the overall philosophy and style of this company?**
  You should be able to get a feel for this through your reading and
  digesting its Web site; and reading its "About Us" and maybe
  uncovering a mission statement. You should be able to pull articles
  about the company (which might include employee quotes), which
  can give you a sense for who they are as well.

- **What is my contact's title and function?** That is, what does she
  do? (Don't be caught unprepared on this most basic piece of
  information.) This should be on the Web site; but if it's not, at
  least ensure that you know the division she works in so that you
  have a general grasp of her skill sets and day-to-day duties.

- **How does this company make money?** This means more than
  knowing what it sells or builds; it means understanding the key
  drivers of the business. How is the company doing in terms of its
  financial outcomes, its reputation, and its growth? This is the most
  important question, but sometimes the hardest to uncover from
  the outside looking in. If it's a public company, you can get it from
  its annual report. If it's a private company, you have to use common
  sense based on what it services or sells.

  Whether the organization is public or private, spend the time necessary
  to think through the challenges faced in this industry—for
  example, hedging fuel costs if you are pursuing a career in aviation,
  increased demand pressures from China if you are pursuing a
  career in mining, or the impact of Sarbanes-Oxley if you are pursuing
  a career in public accounting. You must know the issues of
  your field.

- **Who is this company's ideal client?** As you digest what it does
  and attempt to understand its revenue sources, you should be able
  to recognize trends and commonalities in order to understand its
  most important and most ideal clients.

- **Who are its key competitors?** This is easy! Who else might you
  consider working for?

And perhaps most important two questions:

- **Who am I? And what do I want to do?** Answer from your heart.

Find Something Unique and Demonstrate Your Understanding

Second, and on a deeper level, use the answers to the preceding questions and your research to find something your interviewer doesn't expect you to know, something unique. This is a critical part of the "wow" factor you want to create. Identify something you can reveal that shows you understand his business in a way that someone at your age or experience level might not be expected to know. This could be a fact he wouldn't expect you to know or an awareness of business trends that would impress him.

When I'm working with a prospective client, that might mean revealing that I know about a low-profile charitable event he hosts. And it might be more than just knowing the name of the event, but knowing the date of the event, what charity the event benefits, who is involved, and how much money it has raised in the past. This is one way to really dig deep and *wow* people!

It could also be as small as knowing your interviewer's career history, or knowing a new client your interviewer's firm has landed. It might be a promotion and change in title for your contact, and congratulations are in order (something you would have gathered if you had been tracking the company for some time and noticing these changes). In the Mark DeRosa meeting, it was as simple as M&Ms.

Here's another example. If you were going to meet with me, you should know which of our clients are doing well—which have won a PGA event, signed a long-term baseball contract, or taken their team to the NCAA Final Four. You must know the facts. An even more impressive "deep dive" would be to comment on how rewarding it might have been that Ryuji Imada won his first PGA Tour event in Atlanta (our headquarters). You might comment on our persistence in staying with a young shortstop as he came back from an injury to prove himself. If you can personalize—humanize—your awareness of our firm by showing you not only know the facts but understand the implications, you will make a strong impression.

You need to be able to demonstrate that you understand *how* the business works and the impact this has on the people who work there (including your contact). Remember, employers are not looking for you to be an expert in your field yet, but they are looking for people they believe can become experts. The best way for you to show you are one of these people is to show your passion and drive to master whatever you *can* from the outside.

For example, a 22-year-old gentleman interviewed with me for a job selling endorsements and appearances for our clients. It struck me when, at his age, he not only knew *what* he wanted to do but shared insight on *how*. For example, when we were talking about our approach to landing endorsements, he said he believed that there are two kinds of sales. First, there is selling to a company in a way that focuses simply on closing a deal. This is a short-term approach. Second, there is selling to a company in a way that builds the type of relationship that provides your potential client with the services that will improve their business. This is the long-term approach that leads to repeat business, not a one-time sale. Now, this wasn't a new idea or insight he had discovered, but this level of awareness coming from a 22-year-old showed me he was thinking about the type of job I had available and understood the way our business worked. It was impressive.

I interviewed a young man, Matt, who was interested in a public relations position with us. We were looking to hire someone to help create exposure for our clients via the local, regional, and national media outlets. When we met, he sat on the edge of his seat, and at appropriate times proceeded to tell stories and give examples of how he would position specific players with the media based on their existing situations.

It was clear to me that Matt knew our client list and the needs of each client. He also knew what kind of person we needed for the job, and by telling the stories he did, I could see he would be able both to pitch stories to the media and work directly with our clients. He was polite and respectful as he weaved stories about how he would do this job. He wowed me not only with specific examples but also with his knowledge and relationship skills, which for age 22 were intensely impressive. When Matt walked into my office, he had done his research, he was prepared, he had a goal for the interview, and he impressed me. He got the job.

I must be prepared in my job, too. When I have a meeting with an athlete I want to represent, I learn everything I can before our first talk. I learn everything from his batting average to the name of his girlfriend or wife and even his favorite beverage. Although you might not need the level of personal information I need, you must be prepared for anything.

By hitting an interviewer with a "wow" factor, you do two things. First, you gain respect because she knows you are prepared and you did your research. Second, you set yourself apart from the other hundreds of people she might encounter. It's the intangible qualities that make people say "*wow!*" and that separate you from everybody else.

Wrapping Up and Moving On

Sell yourself and your intangibles, not just your tangible resume. Next you'll learn how to make the first moves toward your career in a fearless way.

Tool Two: Your Fearlessness

CHAPTER 6

Taking Your First Steps onto the Field

Once you have found your passion, you have to demonstrate it fearlessly. No one is going to hand you your dream career. You have to pursue it. And that requires courage and confidence.

Fear is humankind's greatest enemy. But confidence will help you overcome it. Being fearless is not as easy as it sounds. No one wants to fail; no one wants to be exposed or embarrassed. No one craves rejection. During a job search, we all have a fear of being turned down for a position.

For most of us, the fear of failure is manageable; and if it isn't for you, I'll teach you how to manage it. Jeff Francoeur, Gold Glove right fielder for the Braves, knows that if he strikes out in his first at-bat, he still has to step right back into the batter's box at his next at-bat. And before he does, he'll visualize a great swing with solid contact. He knows that taking good swings, being prepared, and sending positive messages to himself will lead to success.

The fear of failure leads some of us to feel anxious or worried. In an interview, we trip over our words and have that "deer in the headlights" look. Every athlete and coach has had that look at some point in his or her life—a coach's first game in a new arena, a PGA Tour player's first tour event, the first at-bat for a player after being called up to the big leagues. The best of the best find a way to dig deep and pull out what it takes to manage the situation in a positive way. That's what *you* must do.

This chapter acknowledges the types of fears that hold people back in their careers and presents a system for overcoming them.

Fear's Vicious Cycle

If you let your fear of rejection and the unknown get out of control, it can paralyze you. Don't let fear cause you to never take any chances or risks. Don't let fear suffocate your confidence.

Embracing challenges is how you get to the next level. It's how you build confidence. You must embrace adversity and do *something!* You can't sit back and do *nothing* in the strange belief that it would be better to forego possible success in order to avoid possible failure. The easy thing isn't the right thing. It's easier to sit back and do nothing than to take a chance on getting hurt or losing. You must pursue what you want and push yourself outside your comfort zone. Otherwise, down the road, you might find yourself in an unsatisfying job, living what Henry David Thoreau wrote about as "lives of quiet desperation."

It's amazing the domino effect of negatives that fear will have on your career. Fear limits you and puts you in a box; these boundaries elicit compromise and mediocrity. And along the way you lose your confidence.

The box you allow fear to put you in limits your exposure. You don't want to make that tough phone call. You are scared to ask for advice. So, in turn, your lack of exposure to people who can help you leads to fewer opportunities. You have avoided hearing "no," but you've obviously avoided getting "yeses" as well.

Because you are afraid of exposing yourself, you end up settling. You fall into a trap of settling for what's easy to get instead of challenging yourself so you can get what you really want. You've effectively eliminated the most difficult options by lack of being proactive. Therefore, you're eliminating your most exciting options, the ones you're most passionate about.

If you settle, you eventually begin to lose confidence and feel vulnerable. Your self-esteem can plunge if you feel you're not living up to your career potential. Vulnerability, in turn, causes stress, worry, and sometimes even panic.

And most problematically, vulnerability makes you crave the security that comes from not taking risks. The desire to have security can inhibit you from breaking down the walls of the box you feel like you are in to get to your dream job. You fear making that phone call, setting up a meeting, approaching someone for help, or following up with someone you met who you think could help you.

How do you overcome these fears and do so quickly? We explore that in the next section.

Bouncing Back from Fear: Get Over It!

One of the differences between good athletes and the best athletes is the ability to embrace challenges as well as recover from adversity quickly. Sports psychologists talk to our athletes about the importance of recovering quickly from adversity, about not letting the negatives from the past influence the future. John Smoltz, longtime pitcher for the Atlanta Braves, has to be able to bounce back from issuing a walk (his version of hearing a "no") to strike out the next batter (a clear "yes"). On a bigger scale, he has to come back from a bad outing—several earned runs in an inning, for example, and getting pulled—to pitch eight or nine scoreless innings on his next outing.

You'll find it's the same in your career search. It takes fearlessness to make those first calls to start networking. It takes fearlessness to walk into the office of someone you don't know and ask for advice. But once you let go of your fear of failure, you will feel your self-imposed restrictions melting away. Fearlessness gives you energy. Fearlessness is freeing. Fearlessness is liberating.

So what does it take to be fearless as you pursue your dream job? You must temporarily suspend your need for security. Quite simply, get over it!

You must be able to put yourself in situations that might make you feel vulnerable. You must be willing to risk hearing "no" in order to get closer to the "yes." You must keep focused and moving forward after hearing a "no" and recovering from adversity. It might help to remember that the process you are going through is something everyone has gone through in their life: At some point, they were in your situation. I answered phones before I was an agent. Everyone has had to climb the ladder—everyone.

Fearlessness Lets You Become Consistently, Uniquely, and Respectfully Persistent

To make the phone calls, to approach people, and to make yourself memorable to people in a classy way takes fearlessness. It takes courage to walk up to someone you think you admire or someone who you think could help you and ask for advice. It takes confidence to be a little different. It takes persistence to send an e-mail a week after she doesn't return your phone call. And it takes great style to do it all in a respectful way so as to ensure that, in the end, the person will like you and respect you enough to want to help you. Of course, you can't do any of this if you're still letting your fears hold you back.

If you can do this, you will fearlessly start closing the relationship gap.

I've been particularly attentive to the importance of fearlessness in the process of closing the relationship gap because I had to do this to meet Lonnie Cooper. I continue to do this when I'm building relationships with some of the most famous and well-recognized talent on the planet. It takes fearlessness to bridge the gap between me and a world-class athlete and then help him see that our agency can best meet his needs (and exceed his every expectation).

For me, fearlessness means acting on my confidence in myself and the quality of our agency. Fear doesn't exist when I reach out to a superstar because I know we can help him capitalize on his window of time as a coach, athlete, or broadcaster. That means I have no fear when I sit in our boardroom with a big-time coach whom we are meeting with about representation or an all-star baseball player who is looking for new representation. That means I have no fear when I call a PGA Tour veteran or head coach in the NFL.

When you have healthy and productive communication, you begin to bridge the relationship gap. You give people information about you, and with this information they are more comfortable making decisions about hiring or helping you. One of the most important pieces of information you can give someone is the proof that you are capable of being fearless.

To effectively bridge the gap with people, you must learn to show your fearlessness by being consistently, uniquely, and respectfully persistent. Following are the elements of my formula for fearlessly approaching people who can help you in your search:

- **Consistency:** Demonstrating your consistency is the proof of your passion and fearlessness. You are showing others by staying steady in your actions that your passion is real, regardless of the frightening obstacles in your path. Aligning your actions—your consistent behavior—is appealing to the kinds of people who will help you or hire you.

- **Uniqueness:** You must also have the courage to be *unique* by allowing your clear and creative intangibles—your passionate style—to show through. There is more supply than demand for entry-level jobs; that is, there are often many more applicants than there are open positions. This means you must find a way to make yourself stand out, to be unique. You must not be afraid to market and sell yourself, and demonstrate a skill set you would bring into the organization that separates you from the competition. Because you are marketing and selling yourself, you must not only show you can fill an employer's niche, but also that you will add value.

- **Respectfulness:** Fearlessness is not foolishness. Although I am advocating bold actions, they must be balanced with my advocacy for a focus on relationships. Part of the fearlessness you must develop is the willingness to invest in personal relationships, to overcome any resistance you might feel about trying to build a long-term point of contact. In other words, take your fearlessness and bubble wrap it with respect and class; otherwise, your fearlessness will be misunderstood and become unproductive. You must be *respectful* by approaching people in a way that leads others to want to help you. Respect is an initial step toward trust and a solid relationship. All other indicators of a healthy relationship are wrapped around respect and trust. Before anyone will be willing to help you, he or she must feel that you are worth helping.

- **Persistence:** Finally, you must be *persistent*. Relationships don't just happen. Finding or changing jobs is not easy; and building a career is not easy, either. You must have the fearlessness to pick yourself up every time you are thrown and "get back on the horse." Persistence is about continually creating opportunities to show that you are committed to what you say is your goal. You do this by persevering through scary situations and putting in the hard work.

By being fearless—and consistently, uniquely, and respectfully persistent, you will be able to drive your game plan.

Wrapping Up and Moving On

Now you've seen the importance of fearlessness. In the next chapter I'll give more advice on overcoming fear in your quest for the big job.

CHAPTER 7

How to Be Fearless

Fearlessness develops inside of you after you have embarked on situations to find the outcome was a success. It develops by pushing yourself to do things that are scary to you, but you know could help you grow, so you do them anyway. And as you do things and do them with success, fearlessness will find a home in you.

Fear is a common feeling that runs through your body when you have to make an important phone call or walk into a boardroom for an important meeting. But the more you put yourself in those types of situations and execute successfully, the fear dissolves and you become fearless. People are often afraid of public speaking, but as they continue to put themselves in those situations—and continue to deliver better and better speeches in front of groups—they begin to approach public speaking with fearlessness. A baseball player is fearful when he takes his first at-bat in the big leagues, but the more and more successful at-bats he has, the more fearless he becomes in his approach to hitting.

As you instill fearlessness in yourself, it will require constant strengthening and development. Two techniques that the pros use to overcome their fears are positive imaging and positive self-messaging.

Positive Imaging

Athletes use visualization constantly. As a tennis player in college, I used to sit in a quiet spot in the locker room and visualize my match before it started. I visualized walking out on the court and greeting my opponent. I would visualize a good warm-up with relaxed strokes and great footwork. Then I would play the entire match in my mind. I always tried to know my opponent's strengths and weaknesses so that my mental match would tap into that information. I always won every point. I visualized her final ball flying out or into the net and me walking up to the net to politely shake her hand.

Ryuji Imada spent time visualizing a win prior to his first tee shot in May 2008 at the AT&T PGA Tour event. John Smoltz visualizes throwing strikes before he runs out to the mound. Positive imaging in your mind can help suffocate your fears and feed success.

Before big meetings and important phone calls, you can overcome your fears by creating positive images in your mind. If it's a meeting, visualize a positive greeting with your contact, a firm handshake, and a confident walk to his office for a meeting. If it's a phone call, walk through the call in your mind before you pick up the phone. Put together your script before you dial and guide the conversation to the outcome you want—the other person accepting your meeting request and giving you her advice and support.

Send Yourself the Right Message

How do you feel when you ask yourself questions such as the following:

- What if they don't ever call me back?
- What if they don't think I'm good enough?
- Where has my confidence gone?
- How come no one wants to hire me?
- Will they be impressed?
- Am I good enough?

Probably not good. Probably a pit opens in your stomach and a shot runs down your spine.

John Smoltz wouldn't be one of the few pitchers in baseball history to strike out 3,000 batters if he walked on the mound and asked himself questions such as the following:

- What if I walk this guy?
- What if I load the bases?
- What if can't strike him out?
- Can I play at this level?

He probably never would have made the big leagues if he told himself things such as the following:

- I don't want the ball.

- I don't belong in the big leagues.

- I can't do this.

John doesn't think this way. Instead, he doesn't doubt himself. He doesn't allow fear to overcome his confidence. John sends himself positive messages, which physiologically relaxes the body so as to allow him to retain his normal throwing motion and throw strikes.

How do you feel when you send yourself positive messages such as the following:

- This company needs me.

- I can make this place better.

- I can make a difference in their bottom line.

- These guys are going to like me.

- I am going to nail this meeting.

- I am prepared, so I am relaxed and confident.

You need confidence. The best athletes, coaches, and broadcasters have it when the lights go on, and so must you. Confidence produces good execution. Good execution secures results.

Wrapping Up and Moving On

Now you have some positive techniques. Practice them to work past your fears. In the next section, you'll start to put together your game plan.

Tool Three:
Your Game Plan

CHAPTER 8

Presenting Your Tangibles: Resumes and Cover Letters

Players in the big leagues get the best equipment—the newest spikes, gloves, and custom-made bats—every season. PGA Tour players have perfectly fitted clubs, club weights, and their choice of balls. But it isn't the equipment that makes them big-league players or the world's best golfers. Having the best equipment might help you *look* professional, but it won't help you actually *play* better or more professionally. Just like a new golfer or baseball player, you must learn how to "swing" at the big-league level in order to be successful in your job search—both in how you present yourself on paper and how you work your relationships.

Although the *tangibles* on your resume and cover letter—your grades, your experience, and your activities—will not get you selected for a job by themselves, they are still very important because most companies use resumes as screening tools and require you to submit them. Your resume gives you an opportunity to show your stats. You must pay attention to the way you present your tangibles because you want to keep them from becoming a *deselection tool*. Because there are more applicants than jobs, resumes become a screening tool.

The information you include on your resume must not only be accurate and well formed (without typos or formatting inconsistencies), it must be presented with style. Highlight your accomplishments, your awards, and the recognition you've received. And eliminate any mistakes, typos, or grammatical errors that could become a reason for a hiring manager not to consider you further. Later in this chapter you'll see examples of how to present yourself well.

Prepare your cover letter and resume carefully, but don't forget that it's what you do in your face-to-face meetings that will bring you to life and matter the most.

Your Resume

Your resume is the most important method for communicating your tangibles. Because most employers tend to view resumes skeptically (as creative nonfiction rather than the straight facts), you must present yourself carefully. Realize that your resume is just a chance to get in the door so that you can show who you really are.

In general it's best to get meetings based on personal contacts and referrals instead of sending your resume to strangers. In situations where submitting a resume is your only option, however, your goal is to impress the employer or contact enough that he or she will be open to meeting with you.

Potential employers will read your resume—quickly—before deciding to meet you. So it must represent you and reflect well on who you are. It should be tight, concise, and have no typos. Your resume should give clear and consistent messages about what you have accomplished. It should focus more on your impact than simply descriptions of jobs you've held. For example:

> **Wrong:** I was on the yearbook committee. It was a great experience.

> **Right:** I was the #2 producer in the school, selling 250 year-books in 3 months. We increased profits by 28% over the preceding year.

Notice that the wrong approach is vague, nonspecific, and difficult to connect to a work setting. The right approach is specific, offers data, and suggests comparisons to other people. A good resume conveys your strengths and how you've applied them successfully.

There are many excellent books available on how to create a great resume. One of the very best, in my opinion, is *Résumé Magic* by Susan Britton Whitcomb. This exceptionally detailed book will guide you through the process of writing a resume with true impact—one that has the power to open the door for face-to-face meetings.

Following is a sample resume from *Résumé Magic,* written for a recent graduate looking for a job in broadcasting.

SHANE THACKERY WHEATON

555 East Cove Road
Solo Beach, CA 95555   http://www.careerfolios.com/swheaton   (555) 555-5555
stw78@hotmail.com

SYNOPSIS

Dual-degree graduate with D.C. internship experiences, qualified for career opportunities where communications expertise, technology skills, and broadcast background will be of value.

EDUCATION

University of California, Santa Barbara

Bachelor of Arts degree, Communications (Dean's List honors; GPA in major: 3.9)   [date]
Bachelor of Arts degree, Political Science   [date]

INTERNSHIPS

Talk Radio News Service & TalkDaily.com, Washington, D.C.   June-August [date]

Assisted in production of daily radio and Internet broadcasts. Researched Internet sources, national newspapers, and other news sources to assemble show content. Wrote daily news summaries for TalkDaily.com. Assisted with ongoing research on talk-show topics. Highlights:

- Broadcast: Cohosted live, 20-minute daily radio broadcast—an assignment normally reserved for full-time staffers.
- Communications: Covered White House press conferences; posed questions to senior officials and the President. Interviewed guests for *Talkers Magazine*, including hosts of top Boston and D.C.-based talk-radio programs.
- Technology: Updated website with daily highlights of talk personalities, such as Rush Limbaugh and Imus.

U.S. Representative Geraldine Smathers, 22nd District, Washington, D.C.   July-August [date]

Represented congresswoman at hearings and provided written analysis of proposed legislation. Served as office contact for major supporters. Wrote constituent correspondence and franked communications. Highlights:

- Communications: Selected among five interns as media spokesperson for several campaign events. Served as precinct captain on election day.
- Technology: Project managed on-time installation of new communications system at campaign headquarters.

LEADERSHIP SKILLS

Delta Delta Gamma, UC-Santa Barbara Campus

- Social Chair: Organized 15-20 annual events for 100-member organization.
- Philanthropy Chair: Envisioned and managed projects that benefited the campus and city.
- Fund-raising Chair: Introduced activities that generated record revenue.

TECHNICAL SKILLS & INTERESTS

- **Computer Skills:** Dreamweaver website design; MS Office (advanced skills in Word, Excel, PowerPoint); MSIE and Netscape Navigator browsers; email applications (Outlook Express, Eudora); Internet research.
- **Favorite Subjects:** Political communications, lobbying, legal advocacy and argumentation, oral debate, drama.
- **Language:** Basic conversational and business Spanish (completed four years of Spanish course work).
- **Activities:** Tennis, golf, canoeing.

Amplified Résumé and References Online: http://www.careerfolios.com/swheaton

---

Figure 8.1: Sample resume for a recent communications/broadcasting graduate.

Author Susan Britton Whitcomb also shares her "Top 10 Tips to Create Résumé Magic":

1. **Write your future success story!** This is a prime opportunity to blow the dust off your career dreams and fine-tune your professional image and personal brand. Take time to contemplate your life-work and how you contribute significance and value to your corner of the world. Your résumé should be an authentic representation of who you are and what sets you apart from other candidates. Target positions that excite you! When there is passion in your work, there will be energy, creativity, and drive, the combination of which spells success.

2. **Build a brand that is in market demand.** This is the all-important link between your passions and the employer's productivity and profitability. A "branded" résumé should convey a value proposition and demonstrate a fit with not only the skills required for the position but the company's organizational culture as well. It tells recruiters or hiring managers that you are a "fast match" instead of a "Jack of all trades." It establishes an immediate connection with employers and answers the eternally critical question: "Why hire you instead of someone else with similar skills?"

3. **Think green—emphasize results.** Write from the employers' perspective. They want to know whether you can make a positive economic impact on the company—how you're going to help them generate money or save money. You can tell them by emphasizing benefits and not just features. Features correspond to skills and tasks (such as programming, sales, and customer service). Benefits represent results, accomplishments, and bottom-line profit (such as a 12 percent increase in efficiency, a 24 percent increase in sales, or a 17 percent increase in customer retention). Emphasize benefits throughout the résumé to appear business savvy and underscore your understanding of the bottom line. A clear value proposition is essential.

4. **Lead with a sizzling summary to capture interest and control impressions.** A meaty introductory qualifications section can help employers zero in on the three to five greatest strengths that communicate your brand. Be sure to include tangible,

"green" accomplishments (see tip 3) to help substantiate each of your strengths and whet the reader's appetite.

5. **Mirror job postings with relevant content.** Before writing, select several job postings that epitomize your job target. Highlight key responsibilities and results from these postings. Then, diligently weave each of these items into your résumé. (Yes, this means that you must write a focused résumé for each job, not a one-size-fits-all résumé.) If you lack certain qualifications from the postings, strategize about how your experience is close to or parallels the requirements. When writing job descriptions, filter every sentence to ensure that it is relevant to your target. Keep job descriptions to three to seven lines at most (any more than this will make the paragraph look "thick" and uninviting to read).

6. **Separate responsibilities from accomplishments.** Recall from tip 3 that accomplishments are critical. Don't bury them in the same paragraph as responsibilities. Use bullets to set off accomplishments and draw the readers' eye toward the results you have delivered. Remember, when it comes to job search, it's all about them, not you. Show how you can solve problems or serve needs.

7. **Weave keywords throughout.** Comb Internet postings, company newsletters, and current articles, as well as talk to people in your target industry, for terms that will help your résumé be unearthed after it is dumped into a résumé database. Emphasize critical keywords by leading off a bullet or paragraph with the keyword. For example, if "public speaking" is important to your candidacy, instead of writing "Made presentations to medical, educational, and business leaders," write "**Public Speaking:** Made presentations to medical, educational, and business leaders—regularly earned 'exceeds expectations' on evaluations."

8. **Substantiate personality traits.** Prove that you have any traits you claim. The phrase "**Customer-focused:** Selected as primary contact for key account" adds more credibility than simply saying, "customer-focused," or worse yet, "good people skills."

9. **Prune and proofread!** Traditional print résumés should be no more than two pages (exceptions to the two-page rule apply for

senior executives, academicians, and licensed medical profession-
als). Ask yourself, "does this information support or detract from
my candidacy?" Omit information if it does not support. Also,
weed out personal pronouns (instead of "I managed," just say
"managed"), helping verbs, and unnecessary prepositional phras-
es. After editing, enlist the support of a competent proofreader,
preferably one well acquainted with the rules of grammar.

10. **Go for the "wow" factor—make it gorgeous!** First impressions
do count. Your résumé should have the look and feel of a polished ad, with a design that is crisp, clean, and eye-catching.
Consider tasteful use of graphic elements, color enhancements,
or small, relevant logos. Match the résumé design to your
industry—if you're in a traditional field, lean toward a more con-
servative design; if you're in a creative field, a more artistic or
imaginative design might be just the thing. Add as much white
space as possible to enhance readability—greater readability means
you'll get your point across faster. Consistent use of fonts, styles,
spacing, and grammar throughout the résumé will also give the
résumé a more attractive appearance. And, of course, proof it at
least twice; typos will detract from an otherwise perfect résumé.

Your Cover Letters

As with your resume, a cover letter should convey who you are and show
that you are able to make an impact on the organization. Make sure each
letter is personalized to the organization, the position, and the person you
are writing to. So do your research and avoid addressing them to "Dear Sir."

Three things you must include in your cover letter are the following:

- **At least one idea that will intrigue the reader:** In my business if
  someone alludes to his relationships in our circle of business, that
  intrigues me. If you are a salesman, touch on how your relationships could be an asset to the organization. If you are a public
  relations person, talk about some ideas you might have relevant to
  their specific business. It shows fearlessness to put out your ideas
  this way, and also shows you are in their world.

- **Evidence that you have done your research:** It's important that
  you weave in a story, a compliment, or an idea. For example, you
  could compliment her on a recent success that you have read

about or uncovered through your research. Or you could extend an idea—this shows fearlessness—based on your research and something you uncovered, which can help show your value.

- **An example of how you can impact the reader's business:** For example, what if someone reached out to me who played college baseball for a respectable program, was drafted to play pro ball, maybe played for a few years (even for multiple teams), and even spent some time in the big leagues and touched on his relationships in the game? Given the right kind of guy, he would be an interesting hire for us because he could most likely secure meetings for us with big-league guys—not to mention the fact that he knows and respects the game of baseball.

But don't overdo it. You will not get the job based on your resume or cover letter, so your goal is only to create enough interest that your contact simply agrees to meet you in person. Here are two examples of cover letters: one that goes overboard with a "gimme" attitude and one that gets it right.

Wrong:

September 20, 20XX

Steve Kincaid
1234 Dream Street
New York, NY 10025

Dear Steve:

I need your help! And you need my help!

It is tough to find great jobs, and I know someone helped you, so guess what—now it is time for you to help me! I don't have any experience, but I'm pretty sure I know I will be magical for a company. Could we talk sometime about exactly what it is you do for your company. I am awesome with people, so clients and colleagues will really think I'm cool, maybe you guys could use some kind of sales help. I really don't believe I should start in an entry-level position, though, because I got a 3.5 average at a very difficult school. So keep your eyes open for some kind of management role I can fill. You know you need my help!

Call me Tuesday at 123-4567.

Peace,

Molly Fletcher

Right:

Molly Fletcher
1234 College Way
East Lansing, MI 48823
123-456-7890 (cell)
mollyfletcher@yahoo.com

July 15, 20XX

Steve Kincaid
Number One Company, LLC
Senior Vice President of Logistics
1234 Corporate Way
New York, NY 12345

Dear Mr. Kincaid:

Number One Company has a strong reputation for delivering results—140% growth over three years and a stock price at double the multiple of your closest competitor. I admire your company greatly because over the years, I have watched your organization grow despite the challenges you have had to overcome in both your supply chain and distribution channels. Congratulations on all your accomplishments, but particularly your recent procurement of Home Depot as a client.

I am reaching out to you in light of your recent growth and what I believe to be a need for additional support within your logistics division. I diligently watched your company during my college years, and it would be an honor for me to be able to meet with you even briefly to discuss my ideas on ways in which I might be able to support your continued growth. I have included my contact information above, and I will also follow up with you this Friday in hopes that we can schedule a time to meet in person.

Thank you for taking the time to read this letter, as I know you are extremely busy.

Sincerely,

Molly Fletcher

Some fantastic books are available on writing great cover letters. If you like *Résumé Magic*, you should check out *Cover Letter Magic* by Wendy S. Enelow and Louise M. Kursmark. This book provides you with expert advice for writing a cover letter that will grab any employer's interest.

Other Important Tangible Job Search Details

Here are a few other details related to your resume and cover letter that you should be sure to attend to.

Your E-mail Address

It's a no-brainer that your resume and cover letter should both include your e-mail address so that contacts and potential employers can get in touch with you easily. But it's not as simple as just slapping your address on the documents. Your e-mail address must be professional. You cannot use e-mail addresses you thought were cute or creative and expect to appear serious about yourself and your career. If you don't have an e-mail account or the one you have is not professional, Yahoo!, Google, and many other companies offer free e-mail accounts; use these services if you need to, and be sure to choose an address that reflects well upon you.

Here are some examples of unprofessional e-mail addresses:

studmuffin1985@yahoo.com

hotchik2@aol.com

beermeup@earthlink.net

thebigman@email.com

Try something that is less likely to influence the impression you are making, like these instead:

johnsmith@yahoo.com

julie1128@aol.com

robertjones@earthlink.net

ryan_mcgee@email.com

Your Cell Phone Number

Naturally, you'll also want to include a phone number on your resume and cover letter. I recommend that you include only your cell phone number so that you can be "on call" for contacts and employers at all times. And be sure to note on your resume that the number is a cell phone number.

If you don't have a cell phone, get one. You cannot miss a call from your contacts and potential employers. Your cell phone must stay glued to your hip throughout this process. You don't need to buy an expensive phone or lots of minutes, but you don't want to miss the call that offers you a dream job or a chance to connect with someone who can help you.

Even though your phone will be with you at all times, there will be times when you just can't take a call at that moment. Make sure your voice-mail message is articulate, professional, and concise. Anything your friends would find funny (beer cans opening or toilets flushing) is probably not appropriate. Instead, try something like this:

> Hi, this is Molly Fletcher and you've reached my cell phone. Please leave a message, including your number, and I will return your call as quickly as possible. Thank you!

Your Personal Business Cards

If you haven't done so already, create your own business card. You can have them made inexpensively at FedEx (https://printonline.fedexkinkos.com) or PaperDirect (www.paperdirect.com), or free at VistaPrint (www.vistaprint.com). Your personal business card is a professional vehicle you can use to introduce yourself to new contacts. The business world revolves around business cards (and v-cards, the electronic version of a business card). Many busy people will not remember your name or information without this prompt to help them.

Simple and professional is the way to go. The goal here is to create something professional and shorter than a resume, to give someone your contact information and prompt him or her to remember you. You are also giving that person information about *how* you work—an important intangible! A business card sends a message that you are a professional.

Always have sufficient business cards ready at all times. Keep them in a business card holder in your purse or your pocket. Have several in your car. Put some in your computer bag. Always, always be prepared. Don't pull a bent and folded card out of the wallet you have been sitting on. This will convey to your contact that you are disorganized and ill prepared and a person that might be unprofessional during an important business meeting with a key prospect or in front of other employees. Don't be that person.

You can extend the value of your cards by adding a short statement about your skills and goals at the bottom of the card.

Molly Fletcher 1234 College Way East Lansing, MI 48823 123-456-7890 (cell) mfff@yahoo.com *A professional, dedicated marketing graduate pursuing the opportunity to help a sports-oriented firm boost its client base.*

Figure 8.2: A business card with skills and goals statement.

Your Stationery

In this age of e-mail and voice mail, why do you need personalized stationery? Because e-mail and voice mail are very common (and therefore impersonal) forms of communication. You are trying to be respectfully unique, and you must be personal to build productive relationships. So, sending letters printed on stationery is a way to stand out.

You will use your personalized stationery after you meet with someone, to send a brief but personal thank-you note. Stationery is also ideal to use after you make an initial contact and secure a meeting. For example, just send a note to the person you are meeting to thank them in advance for their time. When your contact receives a handwritten note like this, it is unique and impressive. It also makes it tougher to cancel your meeting because taking the time to send a handwritten note suggests the value and importance you are placing on this meeting; in an electronic world, a personal note stands out as a signal of the investment of time and energy.

Ensure that you have classy stationery to send notes to people. Have a stationery store print your name in a simple and fairly common font. Either a fold over or non-fold over card is just fine. On a non-fold-over type card, your name should go on one side of the card (preferably at the bottom or top). On a fold-over type card, your name can go in the center of the front panel. The paper should be white.

Wrapping Up and Moving On

Now that you've polished up the way you present your tangibles, it's time to do some scouting to find people to send them to.

CHAPTER 9

Preparing for Your Audience: The Scouting Report

Being a success in any area—as an agent, in a job search, or in your business—requires preparation. In my role, I've had the chance to see firsthand all the efforts that athletes take to ensure they will perform at their best:

- I've walked "inside the ropes" of tour events with our golfers the day before the tournament begins. They roll putts from multiple areas on the green to help them anticipate and plan for different pin placements they might see.

- I've stood with the coaching staff for the University of Florida's basketball team just days before the national championship game as they dissected film on the opposing team, planning their defense.

- I've worked with one of our big-league catchers, Michael Barrett, as he created and implemented new scouting programs for his team in an effort to ensure that he knew the types of pitches the opposing teams' players liked to see and the types of pitches that would strike them out.

- I've talked at length with Erin Andrews (a smart and beautiful sideline sports reporter who many would think might rely only on her looks), and watched her spend hours and hours preparing for the games she will cover. She is always intensely prepared.

Of course, I do a lot of preparation for my job, too. I have to be ready for every phone call, every meeting, and every negotiation.

Planning isn't just about a few tangibles—those facts on your resume and in your cover letter—it's bigger than that. The bigger piece is the relationship piece. You must also plan how you will form the relationships that will help you pursue your dream job. This chapter shows you how to gather the information you'll need to form important relationships and make your plan for success.

Christi: A Girl with a Plan

A young woman whom I first met when she was in high school offers a great illustration of having a game plan. Her passion, fearlessness, and planning not only secured her relationships with people in the business of sports, but they also helped her land her first job as well. Christi began building her relationship network much earlier than most people.

Christi first approached me when I was new in my career and she was a senior in high school. Christi learned through her parents' network of friends that I was working in sports marketing. As she began to hone in on her own vision to work in sports marketing, she tracked down my contact info. She called me (and she called me herself; her parents didn't call for her) and asked whether I would be willing to meet with her to give her some advice about her education based on her career interests. I agreed and we had lunch. Her initiative alone made an impression on me: It isn't often that a high school student asks for career advice, and she was very genuine, sincere, and appreciative during our lunch meeting.

Persistent Follow-Up

A few days after our lunch, I received a very nice handwritten note thanking me for my time and advice. A few months after our lunch, she sent an e-mail to let me know she had graduated from high school and where she was going to college. She clearly planned to stay in touch with me, because I would hear from her several times a year. And each time she contacted me, she always added a little tidbit of information about something interesting she had come across in sports or that she'd noticed I had done. She stayed "in my world" and created respectable and interesting reasons to connect with me. If one of our players did something unique or special, she would e-mail me. She called to congratulate me on the announcement of an athlete we had signed to a deal—either with a team or a company. She did an outstanding job of staying on top of events in our company through our Web site—reading press releases we post or seeing new clients added to the various areas.

At the end of her sophomore year in college, she contacted me to ask whether she could talk to me about applying for an internship at our company for the following summer. I couldn't guarantee her she would get the position, but I was certainly willing to help her. She interviewed with us and approached the interview with great preparation. It was clear she walked in with knowledge about each individual she was meeting with. She impressed my colleagues in the same way she had impressed me, and she got the internship.

A Dream Internship

During her time as an intern, Christi did an outstanding job. She remained consistently, uniquely, and respectfully persistent. She worked hard, did more than she was asked, and wasn't afraid to give her opinion. She asked great questions. She laughed and enjoyed the opportunity but always remained respectful to others. She took everything in so that she could better understand our company and how she could help us grow. She dressed professionally every day; she always smiled as she walked quickly down the halls of the office.

When her internship ended, we asked her to stay in touch during her senior year. She did just that, e-mailing updates to me and my colleagues with whom she had worked during the course of her internship. She continued to look for ways to show she could add value for us. She sent personal, handwritten notes to people in our company. Whenever one of us called her, she answered her cell phone in a professional manner.

Turning an Internship into a Job

As the final months of her senior year closed in, Christi formally submitted a professional resume and cover letter (with her business card clipped to it) for an entry-level position with Career Sports & Entertainment. Although we all knew Christi and had seen her work firsthand, she still came to the interview prepared.

It was an easy decision to offer her a full-time job with us. Christi had the necessary tangibles, but she also had shown us she had all the intangible skills we needed to be fully comfortable bringing her on board. She had consistently demonstrated that she was passionate about the business and the company, she was fearless, and she was prepared. She had shown that she could execute both tangibles and intangibles as she applied for the internship and as she was working there, so she created an opportunity for herself. Over time, Christi had effectively bridged the relationship gap. She had created a relationship with us that led us to want to help her *and* hire her. You can do the same.

Identify People Who Can Help

Your goal is to close the relationship gap. Your first steps in creating the kind of relationships where people want to help or hire you are these:

1. Identifying people who can help you with advice and referrals.

2. Meeting with those people to expand your network of contacts.

When you identify the people you believe will help you, you'll build a list of two different types of people: people you know and people you don't know. In the end, your list will be made up in part of existing relationships (people you know) and in part of people you don't know who have the types of careers you want to have. In other words, the people you identify don't need to be people who have job openings for you. They do need to be people who can be influential and who might have great relationships themselves. They can be inside or outside your area of interest.

You want people on your list who know (and are liked by) people who can help you. These people might have the most influential, high-profile careers. They might, but they might also simply have great relationships and connections. Did you know that the vice president of a Fortune 500 company and a limo driver could have a similar list of contacts? Erv, a limo driver in Chicago whom we frequently hire to drive some of our biggest clients and athletes in that city, has a great personal style and has made friends with many of the people he has chauffeured, so much so that people call him "Ervybody" because they say he knows "every body." It's possible that a relationship with someone like Erv could prove as helpful as a relationship with someone like a VP at a Fortune 500 company.

As you approach people, first and foremost, it is important to know as much about their reputations as you can beforehand. You need to try to uncover whether they are solid and reputable people. I always ask Ryuji Imada about another tour player or John Smoltz about a baseball player before I have any dialogue with someone who might sign with us. Our clients are family and we are all protective of the kinds of people we bring into "the family."

If someone refers you to others, you could be associated with them; therefore, it's important to try to know a little about them before word travels that you have met with them. Ask your contact a few questions about the individual; what does she do? How do you know her? How long has she been with the company? Through the answers, you should get a feel for her. If she is an executive in an organization, you might be able to pull some articles, read her quotes, and get a feel for her that way as well.

When and if you actually meet with a new person, take the information you have learned from others and combine it with your own impressions to form your own judgment. Trust your gut about them.

Starting Your Network

Let's get more specific. To build your own list, first identify at least 10 people you know whom you can use to start your network. Begin by identifying people in your personal sphere. The bigger the list you can put together, the better, but get at least ten people on the list. You can write their names here:

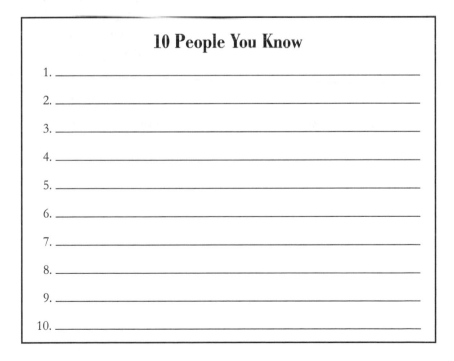

10 People You Know

1. _____

2. _____

3. _____

4. _____

5. _____

6. _____

7. _____

8. _____

9. _____

10. _____

This list might be filled with people in your family, people at your church, or faculty and staff from your college. You've been to your friends' houses, you've met their parents, and maybe you've even met their parents' friends. You can include your professors, your pastor, or your physician. Talk with your parents about their business connections. Talk to your friends about who they or their relatives might know. Do everything you can to build as big a list as possible. And remember, the goal is primarily to find influential people who most likely have built strong and reputable relationships and can support your effort directly or with introductions.

Now, take some time to identify people who hold your dream job now or people who influence those in your dream career. It doesn't matter whether you know them or know how to connect to them. For now, add another 10 people you believe are very close to the work you want to be doing. These can be people in the job you want, or those who have contact with people in the job you want. For example, if you want to be a sports agent, putting me on the list is good, but so is getting a meeting with someone who works for an equipment manufacturer such as Nike or Adidas. If you want to be a Wall Street investment banker, putting the heads of each of the major banks on your list is good, but so is getting a meeting with people working on the trading floors. Get as specific as you can, keeping in mind that even people who work very closely with people in your dream career are a great option.

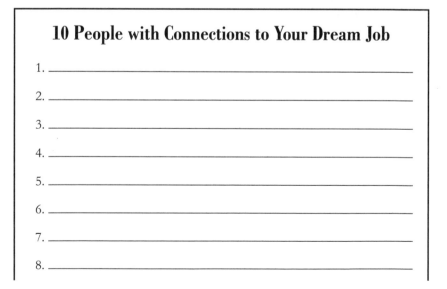

10 People with Connections to Your Dream Job

1. _____

2. _____

3. _____

4. _____

5. _____

6. _____

7. _____

8. _____

9. _____

10. _____

Expanding Your List

At this point, it might seem impossible or intimidating to get in front of some of the people on your second list. Don't worry—stay fearless.

You must be ready to ask each person on your list for three additional contacts with people they respect. Think how quickly your network grows when you ask each of your contacts for three more contacts.

If you are successful in gaining three new referrals from the 10 people on your first list that you know, you now have a list of 40 people in your network: 10 you've met and 30 new contacts. If you are successful in meeting with all 30 and gaining three new referrals from each, you now have a whopping 130 people in your network. By your second round of meetings, you have now connected with 130 people and have at least 130 people helping you—130 agents of your own! (By the way, if you go a third step and get three referrals from each of these, you now have 400 people in your network! And if you've had equal success with your list of people you don't know, you could have 800 contacts.)

But you can't simply sit back and wait for these people to find you a job. This is why you have to stay focused on continuing to get in front of great people and getting them to like and respect you enough to want to help you or hire you. You don't know which of these people will prove to be most beneficial to you, so you must treat each and every one as if he is the most critical relationship in your job search.

You might get your job from the 11th person you meet with, or the 78th, or maybe even the 4th, but the truth is that the quicker you expand your contact base, the quicker you will be talking to people who can help you or hire you.

Four Types of Meetings

In the next chapter, I'll show you how to set up your meetings. For now, here is a rundown of the different types of meetings you might have:

- **Informal interview:** Talking with a person you know about a job he or she has open.

- **Advice meeting:** Talking with a person you know who has no job available.

- **Professional advice meeting:** Talking with someone you don't know but who has a job available.

- **Formal interview:** Meeting with someone you don't know about a specific job that is available.

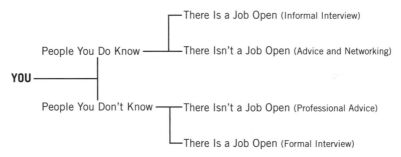

Figure 9.1: The different types of meetings.

Which Types of Interviews Are Most Important?

Don't judge your success by how many formal interviews you secure early on. In fact, the more "advice"-type meetings you can secure, the quicker you will close the relationship gap and navigate toward your dream job.

Most people think about formal interviews as the primary avenue for finding a job, and believe their resumes are the best tools for closing the gap that separates them from their dream jobs. My philosophy is based on using all four types of meetings, but recognizes that you must change your style slightly for each kind of meeting. You should approach a formal interview with someone you know differently than you would approach a formal interview with someone you don't know. And you would approach an information meeting with someone you know and someone you don't know differently.

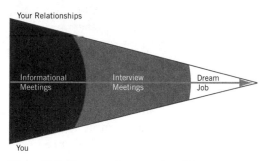

Figure 9.2: How meetings turn into jobs.

Selling Versus Telling

One key difference between the way to approach each type of meeting is the balance between "selling" and "telling." Selling refers to your open and obvious effort to promote yourself as a strong candidate for a specific job; there is a time and a place for this, but it should not be your only tool. Telling refers to a more subtle and indirect effort to help your contact realize for himself that you are a strong candidate—whether or not there is a specific job available. In an informal interview, you are telling: You are talking openly about your fit for the position with someone who knows you well. You are working together to evaluate the fit. In an advice meeting, you are actually moving more toward telling. You are revealing information about yourself in a way that shows your strengths while seeking information and advice on your career.

In a formal interview, you are selling. You must be able to review your qualifications, and you must also sell yourself more overtly. The person you are talking with is not likely to be coaching you on the process; instead, he or she will be focused on determining whether you are a fit for the job. You must learn how to answer questions in ways that directly put your skills—both tangible and intangible—out in the open.

Of course, in both interviews and in advice meetings there will be an overlap. You will do some selling and some advice seeking in both types of meetings, but the balance is very different. Let's look at these in more depth. Telling is giving your contact the opportunity to hear your story and accomplishments and to draw her own conclusions about your potential. And any conclusions she draws on her own will be much more meaningful to her than those you "sell" her on. Telling is respectful, not arrogant, and lets you build the relationship. Telling is not saying "I'm a respectful person"; instead, it's providing a story about a situation at home, or a key point of your life that conveys how you connect with others.

Telling is relying on a story to demonstrate your intangibles. Stories are a very effective way to communicate your passion and your style. When meeting with an athlete we want to represent, I don't tell him over and over "we negotiate outstanding contracts and make our guys tremendous amounts of money on and off the field." Instead, I simply tell him stories about when we made a pitcher the highest-paid relief pitcher in the game at the time of the contract. I might tell a story about the deal we just completed between Delta Airlines and Jeff Francoeur, or reference various off-the-field deals we have secured for our clients. Not only does telling a story allow you to communicate an idea, it enables you to communicate your style and bring your personality to life. It also makes those things real to others.

Have a few stories in your pocket that convey the most important personal qualities employers seek: communication skills, honesty, the ability to work as part of a team, a clear work ethic, and strong analytical skills. Before going to an interview, you should also develop some great stories from your life that exemplify each of your five tools, and other qualities that match up with what employers want in a new hire. Look for opportunities to tell your stories naturally without forcing them into the conversation.

However, telling does not put you in control. In contrast to telling, selling is actively promoting yourself. Selling is confident, assertive, and direct, but it also runs the risk of making you appear arrogant. Most of the time, you *can* sell by telling. But what is the right balance? Where are you comfortable within these categories and how fluidly do you move between them? That's what you need to be cognizant of and get comfortable with in order to be effective.

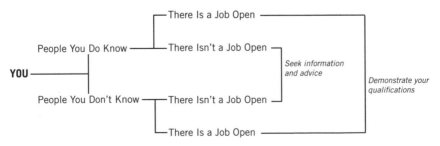

Figure 9.3: Different approaches for different situations.

Tone and Style

Now, think about the tone and style you need to use with each group on your list. Think about how you will talk to the people that you know compared to how you will talk to the people that you don't know. You are probably much more casual and relaxed with those you know, and probably much more formal and professional with those you don't know. That is, you change your timing and your tone based on your relationship with your contact. Instead, think about setting the tone based on whether you know a job is available.

Ask for Advice, Not a Job

For advice meetings, you can take a more informal tone. Ask for advice instead of asking for a job. Why would asking for advice be better than the more direct route of asking for a job? One reason is that most people you meet with will not have a job for you.

A great deal of psychological research has shown that one of the simplest ways to get someone to like you is to help him have positive feelings about himself. This isn't surprising. If someone always feels good about herself when she is with you, she will want to be with you more. One of the easiest ways to create positive feelings is to use your personal style to show genuine interest and concern, and one of the greatest forms of genuine flattery is to sincerely ask someone for advice. Asking for advice puts your contact in a positive situation, whereas asking for a job that probably doesn't exist puts him or her in a negative situation.

In addition to asking for advice, here are some other things you can ask the contact about:

- His or her background

- His or her career

- Any challenges that he or she had to overcome

Questions such as these enable your contact to tell his or her story in a positive light. This seems simple, but it taps into a deeper psychological process that you must understand: When you call someone to directly ask for a job, you will probably make him feel obligated, uncomfortable, and put on the spot. Maybe there is no job available, and he feels like he wasn't able to be helpful. Maybe he is concerned that he won't look "important" enough if he can't find you a position. Maybe he is aware of factors that you don't understand that make you a poor fit. Maybe he has someone else already lined up for the job. Maybe he is worried it will affect your friendship.

Whatever the reason, when you ask directly you are creating an expectation, or a "psychological demand." Of course, how big a burden this will feel like can be very different from person to person. But it is still a psychological demand. Some people will feel happy to help, most people will help and feel a mixture of happiness and obligation, and a very few people will outright refuse you. My point is that when you directly ask for a job, the odds are you will probably create a negative feeling in the person you are asking to help you, and will not get a positive result. But when you simply call people and ask for their advice, talk to them about their own jobs, and seek their views on your career options based on their successes, you compliment them.

The Two Steps of Asking for Advice

To tighten up these thoughts, let's frame them up in two simple ways. When you ask for advice, you want to do two things:

- First, you want your contact to talk about his or her career and experiences in order to help you identify your passions so that you can better understand your options.

- Second, you want to create enough of an impression that he or she wants to help support your journey—he or she will become one of your agents!

Wrapping Up and Moving On

Now you have a game plan, and have built up a list of people you want to meet with (and gain referrals from). In the next chapter, you'll learn the practical steps for contacting people to set up these meetings.

CHAPTER 10

Taking Action

This chapter is about kicking off your networking strategy, becoming your own career agent, and putting together your dream job game plan. I begin by telling you who to approach first. Then I give some hints on how to contact these people through e-mail and phone calls.

Working Toward a Meeting

Now that you have created the lists of people you know and people you don't know, and understand the power of leveraging these relationships into new contacts, let's tie them more directly to your job search process. You are going to reach out to people you know and to people you don't know to learn more about the job you want and the paths to securing it. You will start to network through both your existing relationships and the new relationships you are fostering.

Start with the people you know and the people you don't know but want to. Don't concern yourself with whether they have a job for you. Your primary goal at this point is to get in front of people and get them to like you and respect you enough to help you or hire you. So don't select people to contact based on whether you saw a job posting at their company. Regardless of whether you know the person, sometimes they will have a job opening and sometimes they won't. Sometimes your meetings will focus on how to best approach your job search. In other meetings, you will be talking about a specific job.

Start with People You Know

When you start to build your networking game plan, it's best to start talking to your friends and family first. There are several reasons for starting with people you know as opposed to those you don't.

Where to Begin

First, starting with people you know lets you tell your story and practice presenting yourself without quite so much pressure. There is an anxiousness you will feel when wearing a suit instead of jeans and your favorite sweatshirt, and a discomfort you will find sitting and waiting in the lobby of a business before an important meeting with someone you don't know. You need to learn how to manage yourself in these situations. This is the same reason that many PGA tour players make themselves sink 20 five-foot uphill putts just before heading to the first tee of a tour event. This is why college basketball players often make at least 10 free-throws before every game. As a tennis player, I would not quit practice until I had hit 50 serves in a row without a fault, because the nervousness I felt when I would hit 45 in a row and had 5 to go helped prepare me for the pressure I would feel when I had to serve in a key situation in a match.

The second reason it's important to have professional meetings with friends and family is that they can connect you with people who can get you closer to those in your field of interest. They can also connect you with people who are influential individuals in and outside their organizations. And because they already know and like you, they will be more likely to help you however they can.

Think about the first list of people you put together in chapter 9. That list might include people from your church, friends of your parents, professors, neighbors, friends from your fitness center, and more. Is anyone missing? Are there people you know whom you haven't put on your list? Are you just afraid to sit in front of them and ask them for advice? Stop thinking that! Don't hesitate to put them on your list.

How to Approach the People You Know

Once your list is complete, you will start approaching your contacts to set up meetings. If you are young and approaching friends of the family, they need to believe that your interests are yours, not your parents'. For example, you—not your parents—need to make the initial contact and introduce the idea of a meeting. Remember, everything you do conveys meaning about what you will be like to work with. Having your parents act on your behalf to set up meetings tells your contact that you can't be counted on to do challenging things. If this person is going to take the time and energy to help you, you must show that you are willing to help yourself.

The following sections walk you through the various ways you can reach out to the people that you know.

By Phone

Here's an example of how *not* to call a contact that you know, followed by an example of how to do it right:

Wrong:

> **Molly:** Hey, Steve, what's up man? This is Molly, I'm Ken and Mary's daughter.

> **Steve:** Of course. How are you Molly?

> **Molly:** I'm doing great. I just got back from spring break. It was crazy! We were down in Mexico and had a really big time.

> **Steve:** Well, good, I'm glad you are back safely. (pause)

> **Molly:** So, anyway my dad and mom have been on me about figuring out what I want to do after I graduate, and they really wanted me to call you.

> **Steve:** Okay.

> **Molly:** So, anyway, I'm curious if I could come over one afternoon, or whatever, and spend some time with you. We could talk about job stuff. And I can get my parents off my back!

> **Steve:** Well, sure Molly, anything for you. How about Tuesday at 10 a.m.?

> **Molly:** Cool! You are the man. I'll be there. Wait, where is your office?

Right:

> **Molly:** Hello, Steve, how are you? This is Molly Fletcher, I'm Ken and Mary's daughter.

> **Steve:** Molly, I'm fine, thanks. How are you?

Molly: I'm terrific. I know how busy you must be, so I'll be brief. As you might remember, I'm a junior at Michigan State and I'm beginning to build my job search strategy as I approach graduation. I have some ideas about what I am passionate about and what interests me. I really would like your advice about my career goals.

I'm curious as to whether I can buy you a cup of coffee or lunch, or meet at your office. I know I could really benefit from your point of view.

Steve: Well, I'd be happy to share my thoughts if it will help you. What are you thinking of doing?

Molly: That's what I'd like to talk to you about in more depth. My major is business, but I'm most interested in the business of sports. I know you work in plastics, but I still think your experience would be very helpful to me.

Steve: Great. What about next Tuesday at my office? I'm free at 10 a.m.

Molly: That's perfect. I'll plan on meeting you there. Thank you so much. I'll see you Tuesday.

Notice that I didn't ask for directions. Remember, never ask your contact for information you can find on your own. Even in your first contact, you can communicate something intangible (in this case, that you are proactive and resourceful). If you need directions, either call the receptionist to get the office address or secure the address from the organization's Web site and find the directions online. However, if your contact offers you directions or an address, take them.

By Letter

Frankly, don't send a letter to someone you know. A phone call is much more personal. If you just can't reach someone on the phone, send an e-mail. The following section gives an example of this type of e-mail.

By E-mail

An e-mail is less personal than a phone call. But if you are having trouble connecting with someone, it can be effective. Remember, no matter how well you know this person, you must appear professional and polished in your communication. What you say and how you say it shows what you will be like in a work environment.

Wrong:

> *Dear Steve,*
>
> *Go Green! Big-time win over UM, huh? Hey, listen, curious if I can meet with you on Tuesday or Thursday before noon to get your big thoughts about where I can find a job. My folks have been on me about getting my act together before I graduate. If you can hook me up, even better! So, let me know. Cheers!*
>
> *Molly*

Right:

> *Dear Steve,*
>
> *I hope all is well. Congratulations on Michigan State's win over Michigan. I'm sure that was fun to see in person, and I hope you enjoyed it.*
>
> *I am writing to you to inquire whether you have 30 free minutes in the near future. As you know, I am a junior at Michigan State, and as I approach graduation I am beginning to hone in on my career goals. Your advice and insights would be very helpful to me. I can meet anytime on Tuesday or Thursday. If these days do not fit your schedule, though, I will arrange to meet you at a time that is best for you.*
>
> *Thank you in advance for your advice. I look forward to seeing you.*
>
> *Sincerely,*
>
> *Molly Fletcher*

Taking Action with People You Don't Know

In the preceding section, you saw how to make connections with people you know. But, my experience has shown that you are more likely to find the first job of your career through someone you don't know (yet) but can connect with using my strategy.

So how do you bridge the relationship gap between the people you know and those you don't? In your meetings with the people you know, ask for additional contacts (we'll talk further about these meetings in the next part of this book). Talk to those contacts and then ask them to refer you to even more contacts.

Your first encounter with anyone that you don't know is the most important, the most difficult, and the most intimidating. This is where your passion and creativity will begin to separate you from everybody else. This is when digging deeper matters—and creating opportunities to wow your contact is imperative.

But how do you make that initial contact?

How to Contact People You Don't Know

Early in my career as a sports agent, it was a challenge to approach some of the world's most elite athletes, in a sport I never played, to show them how I could add value to their careers. The more baseball games I attended, the more baseball scouts I spoke with and the more time I spent with veterans like John Smoltz—the more comfortable and reassured I felt that I fit in this space of professional sports. My conversations with NBA coaches like Doc Rivers or Lenny Wilkens became comfortable and well received. But it was anchored around respect; these guys respected me because I was always prepared and I always knew something about their world they didn't think an up-and-coming female agent should know. My confidence developed and a phone call or meeting with Tom Izzo, Jeff Francoeur, or Erin Andrews became as easy for me as a routine overhead in a tennis match. Some 200 clients later, it's no longer hard for me to approach people. And over time, you will feel more confident with the process, too. But those first few can be tough.

There are several ways to make the first contact. The following sections give details and tips on each method. Let's start with the phone call.

The Initial Phone Call

Making a verbal and personal request for someone's time is the best way to ask for your first meeting. You know that your goal on the phone is to make the person like and respect you as quickly as possible. That means he or she must be intrigued enough with your drive and passion to be willing to carve out 15 minutes for you from a busy schedule.

In some cases, you might be able to have someone you know give you an introduction to the new contact before you call. If this isn't possible, you should have something in your pocket that will "wow" your new contact quickly. Based on your research regarding the person you're contacting and his or her firm, you should have something you have discovered that calls for congratulations. Maybe this person was recently promoted or maybe his or her firm just secured a new piece of business. Maybe you can mention something you read on the company's Web site in the "press release" section. Let contacts know you are aware of their world and their recent happenings, and start the conversation with something positive.

You must walk the fine line between being fully professional and very personable at the same time. You want to get to your point across fairly quickly but also show your contact that you are interested in him or her.

Don't pick up the phone until you're sure of what you are going to say. Sometimes it helps to have notes or a script handy. If you are not certain you can stand out from anyone else who might call and be positive, poised, and concise, practice until you're ready.

Here's an example of the wrong way to handle this type of call, followed by the right way:

Wrong:

> **Steve:** Hello?

> **Molly:** Hey, Mr. Kincaid, this is Molly Fletcher. How are you?

> **Steve:** Uh, fine, thanks. How can I help you?

> **Molly:** Yeah, Jim West told me to call you to pick your brain. He told me you had made a killing in the business and encouraged me to try to get in touch with you about my own career. No big rush, but I am graduating soon so I am starting to sweat a bit. Got any time for me?

Right:

> **Steve:** Hello?
>
> **Molly:** Hello, Mr. Kincaid, this is Molly Fletcher. Jim West suggested I contact you for your advice on something.
>
> **Steve:** Okay. How is Jim?
>
> **Molly:** He's great, and a big fan of yours. I met with Jim last week to talk about my career interests, and he told me great things about you and your firm and encouraged me to call you.
>
> **Steve:** Oh, that was kind of him.
>
> **Molly:** Congratulations on your new book! I've just finished reading it. It's terrific. In fact, part of why Jim suggested I call you is your background. I'm starting my job search and am very intrigued with your business.
>
> **Steve:** Well, thank you.
>
> **Molly:** I would love to spend just a few minutes with you to get your advice as I pursue a career in the sports business. Your advice on breaking into the field would be so appreciated.
>
> **Steve:** I'd be happy to talk with you about the field. How about next Tuesday at 8:30 at my office?
>
> **Molly:** That's perfect. A quick question, your e-mail isn't on your Web site and your assistant wasn't comfortable giving it to me— could you share it with me? I don't want to take up much time if I need to contact you about something small.
>
> **Steve:** You can use my work e-mail, steve@dreamcareers.com.
>
> **Molly:** Okay, thanks. All right, I'll see you Tuesday at 8:30.

Here's a foolproof formula for making this kind of call with confidence:

- First, quickly mention the name of the person who referred you to make it clear that this is not a sales call or a "shot in the dark."

- Second, quickly wow him with congratulations on a recent accomplishment, a comment on an industry-specific issue or trend, or any other way to show that you are paying attention to his world.

- Third, after you secure the meeting, politely ask your contact for his e-mail address; many executive assistants will not give it to you. You should already have the company's Web address due to your research. Now you will have three points of contact with this person: a physical address, a phone number, and an e-mail address. You can use these to be uniquely, respectfully, and creatively aggressive.

Dealing with Voice Mail

Whether or not you have a referral, there is a high likelihood that you will get voice mail when you call. Remember that everything you do is selling yourself (or talking your contact out of the sale if you do it badly), and every time you make contact you are teaching that person about who you are. Just as you shouldn't call unless you are prepared to make a brief and concise request, don't make a phone call unless you also are prepared to leave a concise, informative, and positive voice mail.

Here's an example of the wrong way to leave a voice mail, followed by a better example:

Wrong:

> Hey, this is Molly Fletcher. You don't know me, but I really need to meet with you Monday. I'm looking for a job, and I want to see if you have any jobs open or if you would be willing to call some of your friends that might have jobs. I think you are the perfect guy to help! (404) 123-4567. Call me. Thanks, guy.

Right:

> Hello, this is Molly Fletcher. I know you are extremely busy and I appreciate you taking the time to listen to this voice mail. Jim West gave me your name [or if it is not a referral: I have watched

your career and admired your success…] and I am calling to see whether you could carve out 15 minutes. I would love to meet with you and get your advice. I can be reached at (404) 123-4567; however, if we don't connect in the next week or so, I will try recontacting you. Thanks again, good-bye.

Notice that I said "if we don't connect." You should *not* say, "if you don't call me back…" which implies that you are expecting rejection. Rather, you should show your passion and imply that you will be respectfully persistent. It shows you don't mind having the ball and will circle back with him if he doesn't call you. You must put aside your ego for the moment and remember that you are courting him. You are chasing his precious time, advice, and referrals. Additionally, if he doesn't call you and you call him back, you don't look pushy because you said that you were calling him back, anyway.

The number you leave should be for your cell phone. Keep the phone with you at all times—don't go anywhere without it! Work with the phone, eat with the phone, and sleep with the phone—and when it rings, *answer it*. Your best chance comes from talking directly with your contact. Remember, you worked hard to identify and get to this contact, so don't miss the call. Most of the influential people you want to connect with are way too busy to play phone-tag with a stranger looking for work.

What do you do if you leave a voice mail but the person never calls you back? Give him or her at least five business days to call you back. It's good to be aggressive; however, understand that your contact has clients, she might travel, or he might have meetings. A second call too quickly indicates that you are insensitive and selfish in thinking that you should become a top priority in just 48 hours.

When you make the second call, leave a friendly message. Don't specifically mention that this is the "second call," or that you "haven't heard back yet." Instead, simply be professional and straightforward in your message again.

If you were referred to this contact by someone you know, you must also decide whether to let your referrer know that you haven't heard back from her referral, or to continue to hunt down the referral on your own. If you really impressed the person who gave you the referral, she will be bothered that you haven't connected with the contact and might call him herself.

Recognize that this is data for you. The fact that he isn't calling you back might also indicate that you have not wowed him and have not created a compelling reason for this new contact to return your call.

One of our broadcasters once called me and said he had a very sharp woman for us to meet. He said "You might not be hiring, but trust me: You'll love her and might create a spot for her." Because her interests and skill set fell to a different division of the company, I forwarded Vicki's contact information to Camille, the director for that division, and asked that Camille meet with her. She did. The folks in my office were very impressed; however, they needed time to think about if and where she could fit in. Our broadcaster was aware of the meeting Vicki had with us and called the afternoon after and again "pitched" Vicki, saying "trust me, she is special." The bottom line was that he cared enough to take the time and energy to "pitch" Vicki to us. He cared enough not only to recommend her, but also to track her progress and follow up after the meeting. Vicki had someone in her corner who liked and respected her and was eager and willing to help. Although we were not able to hire Vicki, her consistent passion relevant to her progress certainly kept us very engaged.

A Second Call

With some people, it might become necessary to make a second call. Here's an example of the wrong way to do that, followed by a better example:

Wrong:

> Hey, Mr. Kincaid. I called you last week but haven't heard back yet. C'mon, please, please call me. I need to chat with you. My number is (404) 123-4567. Thanks again.

Right:

> Hi, Mr. Kincaid, this is Molly Fletcher. I know how busy you are, but I am very interested in connecting with you. My message on March 1 was about a request for a short meeting to gain your advice, and I remain interested in seeing whether we can find a good day on your calendar for a very brief meeting. Could Melissa, your executive assistant, help facilitate a time for us to meet? I'll try contacting her today as well in hopes she can help us find a few minutes. My phone number is (404) 123-4567 and my e-mail is mfletcher@dreamsinc.com. Again, thank you!

By Letter

If you don't have a referral, a personal phone call with someone you don't know might be challenging, especially given the protective role of executive assistants. So more realistically, you might have to use more formal types of communication to reach out to someone you don't know, such as a letter. This should be a last resort because a more personal phone call increases your odds of securing a meeting.

If you do send a letter, there are several key points you must hit. If you follow this outline, you will find that the letter writes itself.

1. Congratulate your contact on his or her success, and acknowledge that he or she is obviously a very busy person.

2. Let your contact know that you have admired his or her success for years (be sincere, but flatter) and that it has been an inspiration to you.

3. Inquire about the possibility of a meeting (or if the person does not live or work locally, a phone call)—15 minutes is all—to gain advice and insight from your contact.

4. Finish the letter with a clear statement that you would like to meet in person (or talk on the phone) and let the person know that you will follow up with a call or e-mail in hopes of scheduling a time.

Here's an example of the wrong way to do this, followed by a better example:

Wrong:

Dear Mr. Kincaid:

Please call me as I need to get on your calendar. I'm starting a job search and I need your help because everyone has told me you are incredibly well connected. My phone is (404) 123-4567, and I'm usually free in the afternoons.

Thanks,

Molly Fletcher

Right:

Dear Mr. Kincaid:

Over the years I have watched your success. Congratulations on all your accomplishments, but particularly your recent presentation in Austin. I spoke with some people who attended the conference and heard your message was outstanding.

I am reaching out to you in an effort to meet with you for 15 minutes and gain your advice. I have always had a passion for the business side of sports and it would be an honor to meet with you and gain your insight into the field. I have noted my contact information on the top of this letter; however, I will plan to follow up with you shortly in hopes I can meet you briefly in person.

Thank you for taking the time to read this letter. I know you are extremely busy.

Sincerely,

Molly Fletcher

A letter like this should be printed on a high-quality printer. Type the address on the envelope as well. Send the letter through regular mail—don't drop it off in person, even if your contact works nearby. Not only is dropping it off in person unnecessary, it can convey that you are either inefficient or very desperate. The same advice goes for sending your letter via overnight delivery or with some sort of delivery confirmation. I love conveying that you operate with a sense of urgency, but in this situation it's too much—and the tracking confirmation subtly suggests you are already making demands. You'll just look like a money waster with an inflated sense of your own importance.

It is imperative that you stay in control of the next steps in the process. Notice the phrasing, "I will follow up with you." Don't make the common mistake of saying, "I look forward to hearing from you" because it takes you out of the driver's seat. Always attempt to keep the ball in your court, so that you are not waiting on the other person. If you say "I look forward to hearing from you" and then you call them again, you look pushy.

Once I received a letter from a young woman who was seeking advice on getting into sports marketing. She did all the right things during her attempt to contact me, so I asked my assistant to set up a 10-minute phone call with her. Sarah and I talked a few days later and she further impressed me. During our call, I said, "If you are in Atlanta in the near future, please let me know. You could meet with the people who handle our internship program." Because our next class of interns had already been selected, I told her there was no hurry. But she said, "In fact, I'll be there next week and would love the chance to meet." Maybe she really was planning to be in Atlanta the next week, maybe not. Either way, I loved her initiative.

The next week, she met with our internship coordinator and impressed her as well. And a few weeks after that, when one of our committed interns had to pull out of the internship for personal reasons, guess who the internship coordinator called? The person most on her mind, the person who most impressed her, the person she felt had both the tangible and intangible qualities needed.

I remember something my tennis coach used to tell me: "You can't get to the ball too early!" No matter what, get in front of people, and get in front of them as quickly as you can.

Dealing with an Executive Assistant

As you know, Michigan State University men's basketball coach Tom Izzo is an important client of ours. Because of our work together, I now have a level of access to him that I didn't always have. In fact, there was a time before we signed Tom that it was hard for me to reach him at all. I would call and get one of several different assistants working in his office. Each time, I was politely, uniquely, and respectfully persistent. What I didn't know then was that one of Tom's assistants was his sister-in-law, who was most likely conveying to him not just a message but probably a little about my style and relationships as well.

Some people make the mistake of not being professional or respectful to the person answering the phone because they think this person's opinion doesn't matter. But you should assume that everything you say, do, and imply to the assistant will go directly to the contact you are trying to meet—and form an impression. Again, follow my basic philosophy and get people—in this case, assistants—to like you enough to want to help you.

You might need to leave a voice mail for a contact's executive assistant. Here's an example of how not to do that, followed by the right way to do it:

Wrong:

> Hey, Melissa. I'm trying to catch up with Steve, and I know you must talk to him multiple times a day. I've called him a couple of times but he hasn't called me back. I really need to meet with him. I want you to relay this message to him? Tell him I'd like him to call me directly, but if I need to talk to you instead, I guess that's fine, too. (404) 123-4567 is the number here. Make this happen, okay? Thanks.

Right:

> Hi, Melissa, this is Molly Fletcher. A friend of Mr. Kincaid's, Jim West, suggested I contact Steve in hopes that we can spend a few minutes together. Jim has told me wonderful things about Steve and it would certainly be an honor to meet him and get his advice on my career. If you chat with him and can find a 15-minute window in his schedule, I'll owe you [chuckle] and it would certainly be very appreciated [very sincere]. I will e-mail you this request as well. I can be reached at (404) 123-4567 or molly(a) dreamjobs.com. I know you are busy, and I certainly appreciate your help. Thank you very much.

Be as direct and concise as you can, and make it easy for the assistant to recontact you. You can make it easy with the type of voice mail just shown and a follow-up e-mail. If you have difficulty scheduling a face-to-face meeting, offer a phone appointment as an option.

Following Up After You Have Made Contact

After you make contact with someone you don't know and have a meeting set, send a hand-written note on good note paper or your personalized stationery, saying how much you look forward to the meeting. This is rare today, and helps set you apart from everyone else. Ensure that the date and time of the meeting are accurate, double-check the address, and triple-check the spelling of the name. Then mail it the same day that you set the meeting (so that they will receive it within days).

You must be thoughtful about the note you send. It will be a permanent indication of your style and your appreciation and respect for this person's time. Here's an example of how not to do it, followed by the right way:

Wrong:

> *Steve, thanks again. Just a reminder, I'll see you Thursday at 11 a.m. Don't cancel!*
>
> *Molly*

Right:

> *Mr. Kincaid, it was a pleasure speaking with you today. I sincerely appreciate your time on the phone and your willingness to give me 15 minutes out of your busy schedule to talk in person. I look forward to meeting with you at your office on Thursday November 30, 2009 at 11:00 a.m. Again, thank you!*
>
> *Sincerely,*
>
> *Molly Fletcher*

Although schedules always change and your meeting will not be the highest priority to your contact, a note like this can make it just a bit harder for him or her to cancel or postpone it. This note also shows follow-through above and beyond the call of duty, giving an early taste of your professionalism.

As an additional wow factor, send thank-you notes on your stationery to those who helped arrange this meeting. In fact, if someone helps you, even in a small way, send a short thank-you note to him or her as well. It is respectful to circle back and let people know that their time and effort in helping you is paying off.

Wrapping Up and Moving On

You understand how to make contact with people, whether or not you know them. But what do you do in these meetings to set yourself apart from everybody else? "Tool Four: Your Flawless Execution" shows you how to make these meetings go smoothly and successfully.

Tool Four: Your Flawless Execution

CHAPTER 11

The First Two-and-a-Half Minutes of the Advice Meeting

You've worked hard to get this meeting. Now what? *You've got to wow them!* The first two-and-a-half minutes of this meeting are key, but that doesn't mean you must try to get a job offer right away; it means you have to use your style to wow them early.

When I first meet a big-league baseball player or a head coach, I don't ask him to sign with us within minutes of meeting. In fact, it's quite the opposite. Instead, I take the time to get to know him better—and for him to get to know the agency, as well.

Here's a helpful analogy. You don't propose marriage on a first date. Rather, you get to know each other and build a relationship. You listen attentively when your date is speaking and respond properly, you dress nicely, and you call back in a reasonable time frame afterward. Basically, you do what our parents and grandparents used to call "courting." As you do this, you must be genuine. You must be sincere. You should ask insightful questions and listen carefully to the answers. But, as we all know with dating, you often "feel" it within the first few minutes when you see your date at a bar or at church or at a park. Within moments of eye contact and the first small talk, your instincts tell you whether you want to spend more time with this person.

The same instincts play a part in the first two-and-a-half minutes of a meeting with your networking contact. Your contact will be making judgments about you based on limited information. You have to be likeable enough that he or she will want to spend more time with you and help you in your search.

The Importance of First Impressions

The meet-and-greet stage of the meeting is so important that this chapter is devoted to it. The first few minutes set the tone for much of the level of connection between you and your contact. It's imperative to focus on creating an initial connection that sets the stage for intriguing your contact enough to stay engaged for the rest of the meeting (and beyond).

The first two-and-a-half minutes are so important because you have limited time before you must transition to the heart of the meeting quickly. Typically the transition happens four or five minutes or less after shaking hands.

Beginning with the End in Mind

In *The Seven Habits of Highly Successful People,* Stephen Covey suggests beginning with the end in mind. Covey means that in order to get somewhere—anywhere—successfully, you have to know where you are trying to go. Artists have a vision for what their painting will look like before they pick up their brush. Pilots file a flight plan before they take off. Golfers use what they call good "course management." And you have to do this before every meeting.

Let me give you an example of this from a real-life story. Recently, I was able to play golf at Augusta National, home of The Masters golf tournament. I will admit, when we arrived I was awed and intensely appreciative because few people have had the opportunity to play there. The National is known for challenging and quick greens that are difficult to putt on. And, of course, there are so many stories, so much history, and so many special golfers who have played at the National.

Over the years, I have watched golfers walk the course at Augusta before their round. They study each hole, they look for and anticipate possible challenges, and they practice putting from various locations on each green. Pro golfers realize that each shot is their best opportunity to position themselves appropriately for their next shot, and so they want to learn as much about the course as possible. They do this all in an effort to be prepared depending on pin placement (the exact location of the flag). The location of the hole changes every day during a tournament. The exact location of the hole changes a golfer's approach into the green. Not only are greens different sizes, they are also not flat. Each green has unique levels, angles, and ridges that golfers must negotiate successfully. Depending on where the pin is placed, golfers may use different clubs and different shots so that they can end up at the front, back, left, or right of the green to get a good line for their putt. Everything the golf pros do is done in the context of what they want to do next. They are not trying to accomplish the goal all at once (although they could hit a hole-in-one); they are trying to put themselves in the best position possible for the next shot.

The first two-and-a-half minutes of any meeting will be more successful if you have created a strategy to approach and win over your contact, just like our golfers create a strategy on how to approach each hole of the golf course before they tee off. Before you shake hands for the first time with a new contact, you should know what you want your contact to base his or her first impression on. You must keep your goal in mind: getting your contact to like and respect you well enough to want to help you or hire you. And that's why first impressions are so important.

Positioning Yourself for Success

So how do you position yourself in the first few moments of the meeting?

In his book *Blink,* Malcolm Gladwell reviews all the fascinating things that can happen in the blink of an eye—the decisions we can make based on our instincts, and how much more accurate these can be than those based on extensive data and study. Psychological research shows there are some things we just appear to be "pre-wired" to understand in an instant. We quickly decide whether we think a person's personality is warm or cold, open or defensive, or friendly or distant. Our first impressions of people, although not made quite in the blink of an eye, are made in the first few moments of our interactions. These impressions are so important because they can be very challenging to overcome once they're established. Why? We interpret all new information through the filter of that initial impression. Additional interactions might help you change other peoples' impressions of you, but a negative first impression limits your chances to have more interactions with them.

Jerker Denrell, a professor at Stanford Business School, has found that when a potential employer forms a negative first impression of you, he or she is much less likely to be willing to have any more interactions with you, reducing your chances to change that impression. In fact, this process can take far less than two-and-a-half minutes. Frank Bernieri at the University of Toledo found that untrained observers watching a videotape of the first 15 seconds of a job interview were often able to accurately predict which applicants received job offers and which didn't.

So the very first moments of your meeting with any contact are the most critical. If you focused your time on building a solid resume, this might seem unfair, but it's another simple, real-life fact that you have to accept and embrace. In most other areas of your life, you have time to achieve your goals; when you're meeting with a contact who hasn't met you before and is trying to decide what he thinks about you, you will have only a few minutes to draw him in and build the foundation for your goal.

When the Lights Go On

As an agent, I have sat in front of at least 1,000 athletes, coaches, and broadcasters (and hundreds of high-level corporate executives). I have always been athletic and played tennis in college, but I didn't go pro. I haven't coached at a high-level competition. I haven't won a national championship and rallied young men together as a team. I haven't hit a home run in the big leagues. I haven't been a sports writer or sat in a national on-air booth as a broadcaster. I haven't stood over a putt that could cost me my job or make me a couple hundred thousand dollars. And—view it as an asset or a liability—I am a woman! So with all this, some would think I should have several strikes against me in the first few moments of every meeting. But, I will humbly say, I am a five-tool player, so most often my first encounters all go well—and so can yours.

I work very hard to get in front of people we can represent or who can make our clients' lives better. Once I am there, I work even harder to make a great first impression. But the first impression I try to create isn't based on how I have had a similar background to my potential client or that we have shared "on-field" experiences. When I am meeting a potential client for the first time, I spend some time focusing on what our agency has done for other guys, but I really bring to life what we can do for him or her specifically. Don't get me wrong: Having the right credentials and success stories is important (whether past business successes, grades, or internships), but it is not what will make a lasting and positive impression. I quickly look for opportunities to show prospective clients that I speak their language and understand their world. But more important, I ensure that they understand what we can do for them.

First impressions fall into the category of "intangibles" and begin before you open your mouth. From the moment you arrive at the meeting location (whether it is an office, a restaurant, or an airport), you are already communicating with your contact. Here are some questions you'll be answering for that contact with your actions:

- Are you on time?

- Are you dressed appropriately? (It's always better to be overdressed than too casual.) Find a way to have a nice suit to ensure that you look sharp.

- Do you appear anxious, or do you appear excited about the meeting about to occur?

- Have you treated the people you have encountered warmly and politely? (Your contact will probably hear about it otherwise; conversely, an unexpected positive comment from someone as trusted as an assistant can go far for you.)

- How did you conduct yourself when you shook the person's hand?

Not only are you making the first impression on your contact, she will also be projecting forward and imagining you meeting her clients, her friends, or her colleagues. If she's not impressed, she won't want to waste anyone else's time and make herself look bad by introducing you to them.

Making a Big-League First Impression

There are some general and unspoken rules about first impressions. Although they might seem obvious, it's easy to forget about them when you're under stress. Being aware of these rules can help put your contact at ease as well as show your maturity, professionalism, and readiness to enter the business world.

Molly's First-Impression Rules

Here is a list of my rules for first impressions. Think about these from the moment you walk into your contact's office up until you leave after the meeting.

- As you get out of your car to approach his or her office, check your clothes to ensure that you look sharp. Make sure your tie is perfect, your shirt is tucked in, and there's nothing on your face or clothes that doesn't belong.

- Greet the receptionist with a friendly smile and pronounce your contact's name and meeting time. Talk briefly to the receptionist in a friendly manner—but don't make her feel obligated to carry on a conversation with you.

- While you wait for your meeting, look engaged and patient. Don't ever appear bored.

- Sit with confident posture in the waiting area.

- Look up and smile at everyone who passes you in the waiting area.

- Learn as much as you can about your contact while waiting. If there are work samples, professional magazines, or framed newspaper stories on display in the lobby, read them! This could provide you with more insight and can be a source of small-talk questions.

- Have a general "wow" item in mind, ready to go about the company or office (for example, from the display area) in case someone engages you in a conversation.

- Turn off your cell phone, and certainly don't answer it if you mistakenly forget to do so.

- Carry a leather (or good fake) bi-fold with a nice pen (not a disposable pen). Don't have papers or anything hanging out of it. Don't bring a briefcase. A briefcase is for carrying current work and is unnecessary for this type of meeting.

- Don't walk in with your own drink. While in the lobby, don't accept a glass of water or coffee if it is offered to you. Why? Because you want to start your impression by making everything easy and hassle free for them. A glass of water is also something you will have to juggle when meeting your contact, shaking hands, and moving to his or her office. But once you have met your contact, feel free to accept water or coffee if offered again. Obviously, don't ask for it if it's not offered.

- Stand up when your contact comes to get you, reach out to provide a firm handshake, and outwardly show that you are genuinely pleased to have the opportunity to spend time with your contact.

- Be clear, confident, and assertive in your speech. You would be surprised at how many people mumble during this first meeting and all through their job interview!

- Be absolutely, 100 percent, completely sure you know how to pronounce your contact's name. If you aren't sure, be resourceful and proactive—find a way to learn the right pronunciation.

- Let your contact sense that you're a genuinely happy and positive person; people enjoy being around happy people.

Starting the First Impressions

Although first impressions start in the lobby, the timer on your two-and-a-half minutes begins once you have moved to the interviewer's office, conference room, or interview room. When you arrive, immediately look around briefly and take note of what you see: pictures of their family, pictures on the walls, or awards in their office. As you sit down in the office or conference room, thank your contact immediately for taking the time to meet you. Be genuine in recognizing that she is taking time out of a busy day to help you.

Remain on task of sending two important messages:

- You are interested in their world.

- You are prepared for this meeting.

For example, you could demonstrate your interest in their world by asking an insightful question about a picture or display you saw in the waiting area. You could demonstrate your preparedness by congratulating your contact on a new piece of business or an award he received that you uncovered from your research before the meeting.

Sit on the edge of your seat, looking toward your contact with an upright posture, so as to appear confident and attentive. Open your folder and pull out your pen; be ready to make some notes. Appear calm—not fidgety—so as to demonstrate your confidence and overall comfort with the meeting.

The Multiple Levels of Communication in the Advice Meeting

Because the first two-and-a-half minutes of the meeting with your contact are so important, you must remain aware that the first few things you say and do are critical signals you send about yourself. You want them to be upbeat, engaging, and insightful about your contact's world.

Although a lot of attention is paid to "opening lines," yours does not have to be highly creative or unique. In fact, something too clever or practiced will seem artificial. But although your introduction does not have to be long and it does not have to be clever, it must be genuine, it must be smooth, and it must imply that you are not going to immediately impose on your contact. Oftentimes, starting with something positive, complimentary, and about him is a safe approach. For example, "Wow, Jim, what a beautiful setup you have here" or "Jim, I really appreciate your time, especially since I know you are in the middle of a busy time of year with baseball spring training." Although this might seem like unnecessary and trivial small talk, it serves two purposes. First, it opens the channels of communication on a positive but easy topic. Second, it gives you a few moments to focus on his interpersonal style, begin to read his signals, and calm yourself if you are feeling nervous (which will happen at least once or twice!). Although this is a "safe" exchange, multiple levels of communication are going on in even this brief first exchange. Things to ask yourself about your introduction include the following:

- How loudly or softly are you speaking?

- Are you keeping great eye contact?

- Do you appear confident and positive about the meeting, or do you appear nervous and uncertain?

There are many other questions that you could ask yourself during these first few moments of introduction, but the most important point for you is to recognize that, at some level, your contact will be taking this first set of data and using it to picture you in his or her business. Again, think of this as your first date and do the types of things that you would do on a first date. Instead of asking for a job—the equivalent of proposing marriage upon first meeting someone—show your interest in building a relationship. Show your passion for learning more. How would you do this on a date? You would ask questions! In your job search, you will ask confidently for advice. Your questions will be about their experience and your career.

Social Confidence: Nonverbal Signals and Talking About Yourself

Your social confidence is your first opportunity to prove that you can handle business challenges. If you are overwhelmed with the meeting itself, your contact will think that it would be a risk to recommend you to other contacts who might hire you and a potential liability to her and her clients. Pay attention to your body language and keep yourself still, including your fingers, legs, and feet. Don't unconsciously mimic nonverbal behavior (that is, when he crosses his arms, you cross your arms; when she leans back in her chair, you lean back in yours). Because he will be reading your signals as well, you don't want any dead giveaways that you are nervous or potentially lacking confidence. You want to show that you are comfortable meeting new people, establishing rapport, and building a relationship—skills that almost every job requires.

When you talk about yourself—and you will need to, so follow your game plan and prepare ahead—tell your story but keep it short. You should be able to explain your interests, your career goals, and your ideal job. You should be able to answer Lonnie's questions ("who are you and what do you want to do?") and do this in about two-and-a-half minutes, too—no longer. Be sure to include the following in your story:

- Basic biographical information (for example, "I just graduated from Michigan State, where I studied communication and played tennis").

- Why you are there (for example, "I am interested in a career in logistics and want to learn as much as possible about your industry. You have a great reputation and I believe your insights could help guide me since you are 'inside the ropes' and have done it.")

Using Your Wow Factor

Although who you are and your nonverbal signals are important, the single quickest way to set yourself apart is to use that "wow" factor you prepared. Say something you've learned about your contact or his business that will absolutely blow him away. For me in dealing with potential clients, this means looking for that genuine opportunity to show that I know the athlete's world. For example, it's talking to a pitcher about "locating his pitches." If it's a hitter, it's talking about his stance, his "bags" (stolen bases), or his relationship with his manager; it's congratulating a catcher on his defensive play and that he is lowest in the league for allowing passed balls. It's letting a golfer know that I know he is in the top ten on the tour for driving distance off the tee.

In your meetings, you must do the same. Prepare several "wow" factor comments in advance. But always, always, always hold back the "wow" factor you choose to use until the right moment in the meeting. If you come out of the gate with an interesting fact about your contact or try to direct the conversation toward the comment you want to make, it looks forced and artificial—and it won't work. Instead, look for your opportunity and use the situation to decide which piece of information to volunteer. For example, in my work, if am talking to a baseball player about pitching, I might throw in that it is amazing that Mike Maroth is a "crafty" lefty who throws around 84 miles an hour and rarely strikes anyone out but seems to sit a lot of guys down. Or if I walk into Atlanta Braves president (formerly general manager) John Scherholtz's office and notice that he has a screensaver of the different holes at Augusta National, I'll ask him "The National—what did you shoot on number 12?" When you can casually begin a discussion—and share stories—with your contact about some experience you've both shared—it helps gain his respect. When you show you know something about your contact and his world, you'll get respect, too.

You will sit in front of all kinds of people throughout your job search (and your whole life). Start getting into the habit of always trying to connect with each one, to show you can understand their world, and—when necessary—show how you can help them.

Starting the Conversation

As you first shake your contact's hand, you should be ready to start the conversation. Do *not* let yourself be caught stammering or tongue-tied during this first interaction!

Immediately on greeting your contact, you should try to convey your recognition, your respect, and your appreciation for her success without appearing to "schmooze" her or snow her. Her ideal impression of you after the first two-and-a-half minutes is that you are a bright, confident, and engaging person who respects her success and honestly wants to learn from her.

Here's an example of how *not* to start, followed by a better opening:

Wrong:

> Hey, thanks again for seeing me. Searching for a job is a nightmare, and I'm tired of it. Whatever you are doing, I'm really hopeful you'll be able to hook me up.

Right:

> Hi, Steve, I'm Molly Fletcher. It's so great to meet you. Thank you very much for your time. I know a lot of people must approach you for advice, so I am grateful to be here and have the opportunity to share with you for a few minutes. Jim has told me such great things about you, so it is such a pleasure to finally meet you in person.

Whether or not you realize it, your contact, consciously or unconsciously, will evaluate everything you say and do in the context of work. That is, everything you do in this meeting will suggest how you would handle similar situations as an employee. You must pay attention to all the signals you send, because there are many levels to every interaction. On one level there are verbal cues—the actual words you say. These are the "tangibles" of an interaction. On another level, there are the nonverbal cues, your body language and tone. These are the intangibles. *Everything* is data. So you must be attentive to all levels of your interaction.

Levels of Interaction and Influence

There are several levels of interaction and influence, particularly in the first two-and-a-half minutes of a meeting. Two informal categories are most important to keep in mind:

- Confidence

- Initiative

There is no "right" or "wrong" implied in these, and the best job seekers fall somewhere between two ends of a scale for each category. What is important is finding a balance, and the best balance depends on the career you are seeking. That is, you must make an honest appraisal of who you are—your strengths and weaknesses—and also recognize the needs, the wants, and the "world" of the people you are meeting with. How do your needs match up with their needs? What do you need to show more of—or less of?

People have the ability to move up and down these different scales, not just during one meeting but even while discussing one topic, asking questions, and responding to questions. Your goal is to stay fluid along these scales and recognize at each moment who you are at your core while staying sensitive to your audience. You must become a chameleon of sorts—but one who never loses sight of your true colors.

Confidence

One challenge is demonstrating that you are confident without seeming arrogant. You need to appear comfortable in your own skin without being cocky.

Here are three words that might describe a person:

- **Arrogant:** Arrogance is defined as unwarranted confidence. If you are going for a sales career, some of this is good because you need to demonstrate confidence married with some tenacity. If you are going for a public relations career, you can't ever be interpreted as arrogant because you could appear to be a know-it-all, which could make it difficult for you to build effective relationships with the media.

- **Respectful:** Respect is more than being polite. It's showing genuine appreciation for your contact's success. This comes through with great eye contact and genuine attentiveness. It's evident by sitting on the edge of your seat. To show respect, provide sincere praise and appreciation. Ask questions and listen carefully without interrupting. If your contact answers your first questions, show respect and interest by asking intelligent follow-up questions about him or his business.

- **Insecure:** Don't be in awe, don't be a fan, don't be timid, and don't be anything else your contact could misinterpret as insecure. Insecurity isn't attractive—ever. Confidence and a sense of security are important and most appealing to your contact because you will represent their company—and he wants that to be done with healthy confidence.

If you graphed the "tone" of these styles, it might look like figure 11.1. You need to be left of insecure but not yet to where you appear arrogant. I view those in the middle of the scale as being in good shape. You have the confidence to run independently, but are not so autonomous that you appear unmanageable. You should never move too far from "respect" because you will not be particularly appealing to your contact.

ARROGANT →   ← RESPECTFUL →   ←INSECURE

Figure 11.1: The Arrogance/Insecurity scale.

Initiative

You must convey to your contact that you are proactive, engaged, and energetic but in control. You must be able to shift your attention fluidly and at the correct times. Words that describe your personal sense of control include the following:

- **Proactive:** Showing initiative and thoughtfulness about the purpose of a question can suggest that you will do so at work as well. Answer the questions you are asked, but also provide additional relevant information concisely. Focus on your intentions, not just your accomplishments. Provide well-thought-out answers and include numbers whenever possible: Say "I was in the top five percent of my class" instead of "I was a good student."

- **Passive:** Perhaps the worst thing you can do during the meeting is be passive! You have worked hard to get in front of this contact, so make sure you cover the ground you want to cover. Don't sit quietly or wait for your contact to start the meeting or move your agenda forward.

- **Unfocused:** Overly active, and moving quickly between topics or failing to answer a question you are asked. This suggests that you are unfocused or inattentive (or even worse, not very smart). This could indicate that you will not be precise and careful on the job.

Graphing the relationship between these words might look like figure 11.2. Again, you want to be balanced—be proactive without becoming unfocused.

UNFOCUSED →   ← PROACTIVE →   ←PASSIVE

Figure 11.2: The Unfocused/Passive scale.

Wrapping Up and Moving On

You've made it through the first few minutes of the meeting and have made a good first impression. Use minute three and everything after to continue to wow your contact and to get him or her to like you enough to want to hire you or help you.

CHAPTER 12

The Heart of the Advice Meeting

As we've discussed, the first two-and-a-half minutes of any meeting are critical for setting yourself up for success. But you capture this success—and do a lot of the real work—in minute three and every minute after. This is where you bring to life your skills, get down to business, and really wow your contact with your substance.

Because you have only a small window of time for your meeting, you must create a game plan for the heart of the meeting. This chapter shows you how to do that, as well as how to end the meeting on a high note.

Transitioning into the Heart of an Advice Meeting

Now that you have done your meeting and greeting, let's get into the heart of the advice meeting. You spent the first two and-a-half minutes allowing your contact to get a feel for the appreciation and respect you have for his time and success as well as your humbleness and preparedness. You showed him that you are worth investing more time and energy into, and intrigued him for the rest of the meeting. At minute three, you need to make the transition to the heart of the meeting.

When you have reached out to someone whom you believe can be a resource for you and asked her for her time in an effort to get advice, it will probably be up to you to move your meeting to the next stage. You have, in essence, called the meeting, so you need to be the one to signal the move into more meaty questions and stories. As a result, you need to be prepared with questions based on your research. You need to have a few more "wow" factors in your pocket. You need to get your core questions answered, while continuing to get your contact to like and respect you enough to want to hire you or help you.

Gather Information

Earlier, we talked about the importance of having a contact like you enough to want to help you or hire you. This is true, but you need only one of the two to occur in any single meeting. In an advice meeting, your goal is to get the person to like you enough to help you. In some cases, your contact might help you by providing information on the field, feedback on your skills, and referrals to other contacts. The "help" provided is to move you a step forward in your search. But in some cases, your contact might find that he or she is impressed enough to consider you for a job at his company. In this case, the help he provides will be a giant leap forward by putting you onto the candidate track. If this happens, you will likely have at least one more formal interview—and this is where you will focus on being hired.

So in the early parts of the advice meeting, you are attempting to understand a few things. First, although you are there for an informational meeting, does your contact give you any indication that he might have a job open at this company? If he really likes you, he might allude to openings at the company. Can you weave in your "wow" factors enough that your contact might start to think of you as a possible candidate for an open position? Can you ask enough interesting and compelling questions to really get your contact's attention? Can you listen and gather data that you can use to demonstrate how you think? For example, as your contact discusses opportunities and challenges in his business, can you react to those so as to provide him with a chance to get a feel for your ideas?

If you learn there is an opportunity at the company, begin to gauge the timeline. Does it fit with yours? Do you feel that the opportunity would be a good step toward your dream career? If so, continue to gather data and identify holes in your contact's organization that you can fill. If not, continue with getting your contact's general advice, remembering that you just never know how and when someone might be able to help you down the road.

Use Your Time Wisely

You will get only so much time with your contact, and it will go quickly. How slowly or quickly you transition to the purpose of the meeting should be based on your contact's available time. Are there moments in which she looks at you like, "what else?" Is there a moment of silence and she looks at you and says, "So, how I can help you?" If she is courteous but glancing at his watch, hit her with your targeted and detailed questions. Nothing is more frustrating to me than when I have an informational meeting with someone and he just seems excited to be there. I think that some people feel like they have accomplished something by just being there in the office with me. Candidly, they have really accomplished nothing, and in fact hurt their cause if they are not efficient and prepared. So if you aren't sure, err on the quicker side of things; it's better for your contact to think that you are busy and have more to do than less to do.

Taking control of the meeting doesn't mean being demanding or abrupt. It means keeping the flow going and moving the conversation toward your goal. No matter how nice your contact is, no matter how much time she says she has, and no matter how relaxed she appears, she wants to finish this meeting in about 15 to 30 minutes. Trust me! Anyone who can really help you is busy—she doesn't make money giving out free advice. Obviously, if she is telling you about something heavy or personal, don't try to take control and move it along. Wait for the right moment to transition, but move it along.

Example Transitions

Don't openly or awkwardly state that you are transitioning to the body of the meeting. Just take the lead in doing it. Here are some wrong and right examples of how to word your transitions:

Wrong:

> Okay, well that's cool about your vacation and stuff. But I would like to move into the main reason for my requesting this meeting. Are there any opportunities here you could help me with? And if not, can you connect me with anyone else who is interested in hiring someone like me?

Right:

> I'm sure Michigan State will beat Michigan again this year. Steve, as you know, I am aggressively evaluating various professional avenues. I know what I like and at some level what I don't like, but I haven't spent a tremendous amount of time in a business atmosphere to get my bearings. Based on my research and my passions, I am interested in [Steve's industry]. I know it will take a lot of hard work to be where you are one day, and I'd value any insights you could give me on beginning to pursue a career in this field.

As you can see, the second statement feels respectful, makes a subtle transition to the purpose for the meeting, and sets a tone for the rest of the discussion. Don't worry that my words seem forced when you read them on paper. Focus on having a smooth transition in your own passionate style.

Be Focused, Show Energy, and Ask Good Questions

Your contact is taking the time to meet with you, so it is important to stay focused on him. Being focused shows that you are engaged and listening, and being energetic shows that you are interested. So with every question you ask and with every answer you provide, convey focus and energy.

Convey your interest by sitting slightly to the front of your seat and leaning forward. Demonstrate that you value his thoughts by having a notepad out and ready. Remember, your contact will view the way you conduct the meeting as an example of how you will do your job and work with others.

Let me give you some examples of the kinds of questions you should be ready to ask. You would like a conversation to develop, and you can kick-start your discussion with questions such as

- What education, jobs, and experiences got you where you are?

- What insights and wisdom have you gained that could be relevant to a young person like me?

- What advice can you give me as I embark on this journey and as I meet with other people who could help me or hire me?

What you are really saying when you ask these kinds of questions is, "I realize that it takes a lot of work to get where you are," while showing respect and elevating your contact. After you ask each of the preceding questions, stop talking! Ask one at a time and then just listen. Let your contact respond. Show your sincere interest in her response. Be ready to ask some great follow-up questions and pull those "wow" factors out of your pocket. As she tells you her story, remember that everything she shares is data for you about her and the company.

Keep the Conversation Moving with More Questions

Once you have started the conversation, you must take responsibility for keeping it moving. Ask interesting and intelligent questions that demonstrate your passion for your contact's field and your engagement with him. Such questions will indicate you're thinking about the job and the company, and will subtly demonstrate your ability to contribute. This is very important, and an area you must think about before the interview as well as during the interview, so be prepared with insightful questions.

Here are some questions (and the purposes they serve) to help you keep the flow going in an advice meeting:

- **What did you think was most important to know when you started in this field?**

  What You Are Looking For: What you need to do and know right now. What someone in your position will need to know to be successful in breaking into this field.

- **How did you get started? Is that typical of successful people in this field?**

  What You Are Looking For: The building blocks needed to be prepared to construct a career in this field.

- **What has been the most satisfying part of your role?**

  What You Are Looking For: The positives you have to look forward to in working in this field, so that you can consider whether it truly sounds interesting to you.

- **What has been most stressful?**

  What You Are Looking For: The negatives you have to look forward to in working in this field, so that you can consider whether you can handle this career or if it will be too much.

- **What have been the most important lessons you've learned in your career?**

  What You Are Looking For: What you can take away and apply that your contact has learned over the years.

- **What have you learned about this industry that surprises you?**

  What You Are Looking For: Data that will help you develop "wow" factors for your next contact meeting.

- **As you look back, what do you think is the most important quality for success in this field?**

  What You Are Looking For: The skills most important for you to focus on developing or showing you already possess.

- **What other companies do you respect that offer similar positions to those at this company?**

  What You Are Looking For: Any information that will help expand your knowledge of the industry and other future connections.

Beyond giving you good information you can use as you continue your job search, these questions send an important signal to your contact. They show him that this is a priority for you. It lets him also get a sense of your style: that you are sincere and attentive, that you are passionate and committed, that you are interesting, and that you are coachable. The bottom line is that this person will not want to go out of his way for you unless he knows that you are working hard yourself.

Throughout the meeting, make sure you ask questions that show you are evaluating the company in a respectful way rather than judgmentally. Provide short, concise, and confident answers to questions your contact asks you. Each should be somewhere between 20 seconds and 2 minutes long. Spend 50 percent of your time speaking and 50 percent of your time listening. But because it is an informational meeting and you are asking most of the questions, make sure it is evident to your contact that you have the ability to take control when needed.

Give Back

Show that you are a self-starter with initiative. Look for ways to show that you can help your contact, not just how she can help you. You might think, "Come on, how can I help this bigwig?" Easy!

- If she tells you she is going skiing in Aspen but hasn't been there before and you have, share insight about Aspen and the name of a great restaurant or some other attraction you can recommend.

- Maybe she tells you during the course of your meeting that she loves country music, but you know very little about country music. After the meeting, find out if there is a country music star playing nearby soon or something relevant to the local country music scene. Mention that information in a follow-up e-mail, displaying your interest in her and your attention to what she said.

- Maybe she shares that the office is full of Atlanta Braves fans and that they are gathering tonight to watch them play the Mets. E-mail her after the Braves' win with a short note: "Hey, I saw the Braves won. I know they were due for it and I know you wanted it. Hope you enjoyed the R&R time with your team." It shows you were listening and that you are attentive to your passion 24/7.

Now *that* is one way to wow your contact; *that* is being in her world!

Closing the Advice Meeting

You need to prepare closing comments that are tied to next steps. Make a statement based on what you have learned. For example, "I'll follow up with you Tuesday regarding John from Dreams, Inc., and Mary from Go For It, Inc. Or, "I'll follow up with Sally, your Director of HR on Monday to discuss next steps."

Be ready to provide a crisp, clean, business card (not one that you have been sitting on for weeks in your wallet). And do this even if you think the interview went poorly. No matter how you feel the meeting went, express your sincere appreciation at the end for the time that was given to you.

As you begin to close the meeting, you should have a feel for whether your contact might be willing and able to help you. And even though you have asked for this meeting to gain insight and advice, during your time together you should have been able to gather whether there is a job available at your contact's organization. However, if he doesn't indicate any specific position in the firm and you believe he seems genuinely interested in helping you, it is still important that you build your network base—and he can help you. How? Simply ask! Here's an example of how not to do this, followed by the right way:

Wrong:

> It's unfortunate you don't have any jobs here for me because I think I would be a great addition to your company. Could you at least hook me up with some people like you who might actually hire me?

Right:

> Steve, you have been wonderful and I feel like I have a good understanding of how you were able to secure the position you hold. This talk has been so helpful to me. Would you be able to recommend me to some friends in your business who might take my call? Whether or not they have a position open at this moment isn't important. I just know the more great people I can get in front of, the more I'll learn about the field and the better prepared I will be for my career.

Your contact should have a feel at this point for the type of referrals you are interested in; however, the more specific you can be, the better. People often ask me for referrals or introductions. There are probably 3,000 contacts in my database, and anyone who asks needs to focus me on the specific areas he is interested in so that the referrals are more likely to be effective. For example, if someone says she is interested in working for an organization such as the NFL, I can filter through the various people I could connect her with in that arena. Or if someone were interested in working for a golf equipment company, I would connect him with people at various companies I work with now.

While you are talking with your contact, you should be evaluating her as well. Sometimes it's helpful to pretend that you are looking down at your meeting from the ceiling. Imagine studying both people, watching the style each person is using, and listening to the tone of the meeting. Does your contact seem reputable? Will she represent you well to other people? Is she the kind of person you want advocating you? If not, it might be best to close the meeting without asking for referrals.

Once a contact gives you the name of another contact, you must ask, "Would you like to call or e-mail him first and let him know I will be calling? Or would it be best for me just to call him this afternoon and reference your name?" Note that by using the phrase "this afternoon," you are signaling a sense of urgency and showing that you are task-oriented. Remember, these people are busy, so don't be so presumptuous as to think that they will preface your call—in fact, many won't.

Getting additional references lets you quickly expand your network and gets you closer to your dream job. As you get in front of more people, you will grow your list of contacts very quickly. You started your list with 20 people (10 you knew and 10 you didn't know yet), and if you were successful in getting them to like and respect you enough to want to hire you or help you, you should be walking out of each meeting with three additional contacts. Your list will grow rapidly from 20 people to 60 new people to 180 new people to 540 new people! With that many personal contacts and introductions, you are one heck of an agent for yourself and you are likely to get close to your dream. And you have recruited many people to act as agents for you, as well.

Keeping these contacts organized is imperative. I recommend Microsoft Outlook as well as software or Internet-based applications. It is simply important to have a format in which you can note the person's name, company, and contact information and make notes relevant to your conversations and next steps.

Wrapping Up and Moving On

You've learned how to flawlessly execute an informal informational interview and manage your growing list of contacts. It won't be long before you start getting "real" interviews. The next chapter shows you how to manage this more stressful type of meeting.

CHAPTER 13

The Heart of Formal Job Interviews

Through multiple advice meetings, you now find yourself sitting in front of someone who has a job opening. The process for the first two-and-a-half minutes of an interview will be the same as the one you used for your advice meetings; however, your strategy as you begin to enter into the heart of the meeting will be different.

In a formal job interview, the interviewer typically spearheads the tone and direction of the meeting, whereas in advice meetings, you were responsible for keeping things moving. In an interview, you need to be prepared to respond to questions, whereas in an advice meeting, you need to ask the questions. Take the attitude that this organization is hiring in order to solve a problem. Find out what that problem is and show that you are the solution. Uncover the organization's needs and give your interviewer the answer to the question "Why should this company hire *you?*"

You've spent years preparing both socially and through traditional education channels for an opportunity like this. But it can still come down to a 30-mintue meeting to put you on track to your dream career.

Gathering Data During the Interview

In interviews, your contact will take control of the flow and tone of the meeting. During the heart of the meeting, you must tap into the data that you gathered ahead of time and use it to respond to the interviewer's questions. And, in a perfect world, during your dialogue you will gather information you can use to better position yourself.

Listen for professional and personal data. For example, listen for names of people she works with. Pay attention to where excitement and passion creep into her voice. Notice where she seems to relax, where she seems energized, and where her body language changes. Maybe it's when she mentions the companies where she is selling services or working. Listen for dates of a big meeting or the conclusion of a key project. Although it is a formal interview, take note if she mentions her spouse or children.

Listen, and then store the data you gather—either in your mind or on your notepad. As the meeting progresses, use this information as part of your follow-up strategy. If you have listened intently and watched for changes in tone, you can wow your contact with a reference or dialogue about something that clearly excites her As the interview wraps up, you can wish him well on his "family vacation skiing in Aspen next week," or you can say "wish you the best with your meeting with ESPN next Tuesday." And if you can, take it a step further in a way that shows you understand the business: "Congratulations on obtaining that event business from Home Depot. As that relationship grows, I am sure you will begin to hire even more people. Congratulations!" With observations like these, your contact will know that you are thoughtful and attentive.

Preparation Is Key

One of the most important ways to be successful during interviews is to be prepared. With the same detail that you prepared for the informational interview, you must prepare for an interview as well. Revisit all your earlier notes and refresh yourself on the key elements of the business. As you prepare, ask yourself some pointed questions relevant to the interviewer as well as the company. Make sure you can answer these questions before you get to your interview:

- What are her day-to-day duties?

- What is her company's overall business and growth strategy?

- How can you add value immediately?

- Based on this job opening, what is the specific hole I could fill?

- What seems to be her most immediate challenge and need?

Much of the body of the meeting will be centered on the interviewer determining whether you have the tangible and intangible qualities he seeks to solve his challenges. You need to be prepared with "wow" factors that are relevant to solving his problems. Also, you'll need to prepare intelligent questions to ask about the company, the division, and its projected growth. For example:

- I read on your Web site that you are beginning to branch out into _____. All the additional information I've read seems to indicate this will be a great niche. Have you locked any clients into that space yet?

- How is your company different than it was five years ago? How will it look five years from now?

- What is the biggest challenge this organization faces today? Is this true for the whole industry?

- It seems to me that your company's primary competitive advantage is _____. Is this true? What must you do to stay competitive?

- What are your strategies to gain customers? (Some interviewers may choose not to answer this question in an early interview or may give you a broad answer on general strategies.)

- What do you believe is the key to long-term success at this company?

- What do you think are the most important expectations for success in this position? What are the most important skills for me to show you to assure you that I can meet those expectations?

- What are the characteristics of people who have been successful in this job?

Setting the Tone

The overall tone and feel for the meeting should remain positive. Work to avoid anything negative and ensure that you've shown the interviewer your passion, energy, and commitment to your career goals. Remain selfless in your listening and your responses. In other words, as the interviewer shares with you, don't redirect each story or example back to yourself. Be sure you present a humble but strong presence about yourself and be sincerely appreciative throughout.

Remain professional and never allow yourself to become too casual, no matter how casual the interviewer becomes. If, for example, you sit with her in the boardroom, never sit at the head of the table. You have not earned the right to sit at the head of the table. This might seem like quaint symbolism, but ignorance of it sends a bad message to the interviewer.

Never interrupt! If the interviewer is talking, simply listen and gather information. If you have something to share, wait for the right moment. Interrupting implies that you believe what you have to say is more important than what he has to say.

As the meeting progresses, reference and tap into the information you have gathered. Listen intently to the tone and level of excitement in the interviewer's voice. Wow him with a reference to something that clearly excited him.

Don't be shy about asking the questions that you have prepared. If you really feel ready, throw out an idea about something the interviewer shared with you. Position this idea as a question. For example, you can preface it with "Have you thought about…" or "Would it be appropriate to…." You want the interviewer to experience exactly what it would be like to work with you. Asking intelligent questions at the right time (which will be possible if you have done your preparation) is what will set you apart. Be prepared!

Typically toward the end of an interview, the interviewer might say, "Do you have any questions for me?" That is your chance to ask your questions—take it. Nothing is more irritating to me than when after I interview someone and I say, "do you have any questions for me?" they respond with "No, I think you answered all my questions." I think one of two things. First, she says she is excited about a career in sports marketing but can't come up with even one question; how passionate is she? Second, he must be scared to talk to me or doesn't want to say something I won't like. Is he the kind of person I want to hire?

Questions Interviewers Might Ask

You have prepared for your interviews and created some "wow" moments for each, but you also need to prepare for the questions you will be asked.

My definition of an effective interview is one where you get up out of the chair to leave feeling that you have successfully conveyed how you are a solution to the organization's current problems and a great fit for its future opportunities. To do this, it is imperative that you prepare to answer all the questions you will be asked. You must anticipate the interviewer's questions and know how you will answer them.

Three Types of Interview Questions

Although there are potentially thousands of different questions you could be asked, it helps to think of them in groups. Corporate psychologists classify these questions into three types, and there is a good way to answer each:

- **Evidence-based questions:** Designed to gather facts and information about your tangibles. Examples are "What was your grade-point average?" and "How did you perform compared to your objectives on your internship?" Answer these questions factually and concisely. Resist any temptation to tell "stories" or go off on tangents when asked evidence-based questions.

- **Personality-based questions:** Designed to get you to reveal something about yourself and your style. These questions focus on your intangibles so reveal something impressive! This is where the difference between telling and selling is so important. Reveal your personality and characteristics, but don't hit the interviewer over the head with them. Tell a short story, use humor, and be human.

- **Curve-ball questions:** This type of question is relatively rare, but because it has gotten a lot of attention in the press, your interviewer might include one. A curve-ball question is usually inserted into the middle of an interview, is disconnected from the question right before and after it, and might require some thought to answer. (Example: "Why are manhole covers round?") It is designed to create a situation in the interview for which you could not have been prepared. The idea behind the curve ball question is that it could reveal how you handle thinking on your feet, and might show how you handle pressure.

Of course, you cannot prepare for these questions and I can't give you any answers in advance. But if you are asked one, keep in mind that how you handle it is as important as what you say. Upon hearing the question, remain still in your chair, pause for a moment, and say "Great question; I need to think about that one." When you feel ready, give your best shot at answering the question. Don't wait too long and don't avoid giving an answer. Remember that how you are *handling* the curve ball is as important as your actual answer.

Answering Common Questions

In an interview, it is critical that you hear, understand, and answer the questions that are asked. Just as there are multiple levels to every interaction, there are multiple levels to every question—and to your answer. To help you understand this, I have listed some common questions you might be asked in interviews (and in advice meetings, too).

For each of the questions, first try to recognize the purpose of the question. That is, try to discern the question behind the question, the motivation the interviewer has for asking the question, and what he is really seeking to understand. This might not always be as obvious as it seems.

You have to answer both the surface-level questions *and* the deeper-level questions in your responses. This is not easy; you must walk the fine line between answering with what you think the interviewer wants to hear and remaining honest and genuine. The answer you give is so much more than just the words you say; it's also all the information you convey while you are speaking. You must pay attention to not only what you are saying, but how you are saying it.

Of course, just like a curve-ball question, I can't give you the exact words you need to answer every possible interview question. Not only would it take volumes to write out, but my words wouldn't be sincere for you or from your heart. However, I can list some common questions that you might hear, along with ideas to help you understand the *real* questions behind the questions and a strategy for your response.

You should be ready for any of the following questions, knowing that you have to find your own answers and say them in your own words. A good answer to any interview question conveys both *facts* and *emotion*. It shows a bit of the person—your intangibles—within the answer. For each question, don't sound rehearsed. Answer in your own words, answer briefly and concisely, and allow the interviewer to ask a follow-up question if she wants to. This will ensure that you continue a healthy dialogue and not a monologue.

Why are you interested in this company?

> **The real question:** How well do your career goals fit with our employment needs?

> **Strategy:** This is a great opportunity for you to demonstrate your passion for this industry and communicate that you have

researched this company and are aware of their great reputation. Don't try to say too much, but be sure that your interviewer senses your passion and preparedness.

What's your story?

Tell me about yourself.

The real question: Are you comfortable with who you are and what you want to do? Will you fit in here? How well do you match our culture?

Strategy: There is no real way to know what the person asking you this question is looking for in terms of "fit"—in fact, one of the reasons that companies often have you interview with several people is that each of them wants and looks for different qualities from candidates.

Because this is a very common question, you should be comfortable telling "your story" before you reach the interview. Have it planned out and ready in advance. Again, be honest and open, and use your own words but think about structuring your response in a way that hits several key topics: your background, your professional interests and why this company fits those interests, and your personal interests. Remember that every person is different in how much personal information he wants to hear. Be flexible enough to adapt your story based on the signals you are getting from the interviewer. It's important to realize that the story you tell needs to help you "bond" with the person while simultaneously demonstrating the characteristics that you believe to be important for performing the job well. If you are telling a story that is too long or too short, you might miss this opportunity.

What do you know about this field?

What do you know about the company?

The real question: How serious are you? How much effort have you put into this so far? Did you do your research?

Strategy: Provide a short, concise answer that shows you understand the company and industry. Start with a broad comment or two about the industry and this company's position within it. Then look for an opportunity to drop in a "wow" factor that helps the interviewer see that you are in his world. This is an opportunity to give the interviewer a taste of how you think. You don't have to prove you are an expert. You just have to show that you are interested enough in the field to be paying attention to it and have enough motivation to do some homework on the places you would like to work.

Why do you think you should get this job?

The real question: Do you really know what it takes? What do you understand about yourself and this industry that suggests you will be successful in this job? Do you have more than just raw energy or enthusiasm? How much am I going to have to teach you?

Strategy: You must be very careful how you answer this question because you are being asked to quickly summarize your personal and professional skills. In fact, giving a quick, obvious, and stereotypical answer will hurt you more than a thoughtful answer will help you. So the strategy needs to be an honest appraisal of yourself, putting much more emphasis on strengths than weaknesses but not overlooking your needs to grow and develop.

Let me give you an example. People often think those of us working in sports marketing go to sporting events day after day—and we certainly attend plenty—but much of our work takes place when athletes are off the field. So when a job candidate answers "I just love everything about sports," or "I'm a big fan," it's a negative in my mind. We don't hire people who are "fans." We hire people who embrace the business side of sports and consistently find ways to add value—to our clients, to our company, and to the business of sports.

It is so important to make sure you really understand and have done your research as to what the company does and the role of the person you are meeting with. When you answer this question, use words like "intrigued by the business," "growth trends," "upside potential," and "challenging each day." By expressing your sincerity based on your research, you are establishing wonderful credibility with your interviewer.

How would you describe yourself?

The real question: What do you see as your defining qualities? Are you persistent, knowledgeable, smart, confident, aggressive, patient—or any other quality we are looking for?

Strategy: Be genuine but cognizant of your audience. You need to be cognizant of the qualities that are required for success in this job, and identify the areas where your own style is or is not a fit. Answer by giving some factual information—your background, your school, your major—and then talk about yourself as a person.

What are your greatest strengths?

The real question: Do you see yourself as having the basic qualities needed for success in this field?

Strategy: Because she asked directly for your strengths, dive right in. Give two to four key strengths you see in yourself and that you have prepared (ones that would match up well with the career you are seeking). But don't give more than four because you don't want to drone on too long. And if you can, tell rather than sell. Instead of simply listing your qualities, work some stories into your answers that reveal these qualities.

What are your biggest weaknesses?

The real question: First, do you see yourself as having weaknesses? Second, how open, self-aware, and insightful do you seem to be about those weaknesses? Third, how easy or hard might it be for me to train you, to give you feedback, or to correct you when you make the inevitable mistakes that come from learning a job?

Strategy: Be prepared: The interviewer won't focus only on your strengths. Remember, even the best sports stars excel in several areas but are closer to average in a few others. Have three to five personal weaknesses ready to discuss. Provide two or three when you are asked, and save the others in case you are pushed for more.

As you discuss your weaknesses, be genuine. Be honest, but don't be too critical. You aren't doing yourself or your interviewer a favor if you try to gloss over weaknesses. You might end up in a job that you will fail to perform well. If you think you will be challenged by the amount of detail needed in the job, say so. It's okay to disclose the weakness. When you do note a weakness, also provide your plan for overcoming this weakness. Identify the weakness and show one or two ways you have worked to overcome the weakness or adapt to it.

Here's something that is very important to hear: You must resist the temptation to claim that a positive quality is actually a weakness. Employers aren't fooled by this trick ("I'm too much of a perfectionist in my work" or "I work too many hours")."

Here's an example of a response that walks this fine line successfully:

"In my first internship, during my sophomore year in college, I struggled with being as detail-oriented as I needed to be because I like to work quickly. This led me to overlook issues in the past. However, I received feedback on this matter and slowed down enough to ensure my work is perfect (say with a smile)."

After answering a question about your weakness, talk briefly—and the key word is *briefly*—about one of your strengths and your interest in this field. This lets you return to a positive tone. For example, adding one sentence to the description of your weakness can change the tone without appearing insincere:

"...I slowed down enough to ensure my work is perfect. Between this change and the strong relationships I build with customers, I'm sure I will be successful in meeting your sales goals."

What type of work do you like best?

What has been your favorite job in the past?

What classes did you enjoy in school?

The real question: What motivates you?

Strategy: Your answers need to align with the characteristics of a person who is likely to be successful in this job. And if you feel you aren't being honest when you answer, perhaps this really isn't the right job for you.

Try to focus on examples from work or school that allowed you to deepen your thinking, show initiative or responsibility, or push for results. Saying you enjoyed your sociology class because it was "cool stuff" does not carry the same weight as saying you enjoyed sociology because "it helped me to see cultural issues from a broader point of view." Saying your favorite job was working for the neighborhood theatre "because of the free movies" is not as likely to impress your contact as saying "because of the responsibility I was given to close the theatre and balance the cash register."

Which of your accomplishments gives you the greatest satisfaction?

The real question: What is the primary focus of your energy?

Strategy: This is another question for which there are no right or wrong answers. But what you say will reveal important infor-mation about you. There are a number of possible reasons for asking this question:

- What motivates you?

- Are you most focused on work, family, or personal interests?

- What type of accomplishments do you find satisfying (and can we provide those to you or will you quit in six months)?

- Did you accomplish this independently or were you part of a team?

- Did you do something new or did you find a way to fix a problem or improve an existing process?

As you can see, this is a complex question. But you don't need to be intimidated by it. Know what you have accomplished, be ready to explain why it is significant, and find a way to show how it relates to the position you are seeking.

What are your interests outside work?

The real question: Is there evidence you can learn and master multiple skills?

Strategy: Whether your outside interests are more group-oriented (team sports, live music, social clubs) or individual-oriented (reading, hiking, collecting stamps), clearly convey the *interest you have* that helps you become *active and engaged* and *learn new things*. Here's an example of an answer that gives just the right tone and depth:

"I really enjoy good, well-crafted, and well-performed music, the kind that conveys the thoughts and feelings of the songwriter. So I listen to a lot of different types of music—classical, jazz, rock—and I'm always on the lookout for new bands. Whenever I can, I go hear a good musician live and try to figure out what makes his music so appealing."

Why did you leave your last job?

The real question: What problems have arisen in past jobs—the best indicator we might have for where problems might arise in future jobs? And how did you handle it?

Strategy: Be positive but honest. It's okay to "spin," but if you must, spin honestly.

I interviewed a young man who was only one year out of college. Here's how he explained this; in a way that didn't work. He had been selling phones for the last year. He was one guy on a 10-man team. The company needed to reduce the size of its workforce and went through a series of layoffs. It needed to lay off two members of his team—and he was one of the two. The truth is, when he told me this, he lost me. He lost me from hiring him (because everyone I hire in one way or another has to be a great salesperson), and he lost me from helping him because past behavior is the best predictor of future behavior. And I quickly assumed there must be some reason he was one of the bottom 20 percent of his team.

If you have left a job—either through your own actions (quitting or getting fired) or not (getting laid off or downsized)—you must pull back before you begin interviewing and reevaluate yourself. Make sure you are at peace with who you are—your strengths and your weaknesses; you must be honest with yourself about your passions and how they match up with adding value to an organization. If you were fired, take some time to dig deep inside yourself and understand what you could have done better for the preceding situation to have worked and what you can learn from that to make your next situation a success. If you were laid off, have an explanation of the circumstances and the size of the lay-off. Don't try to paint it as a "blessing in disguise" or show anger at the circumstances. Speak frankly and honestly about it. If you have quit a job, give an honest answer about the problems that led you to decide to leave—and balance these with the positive aspects of the job, too. Then tell a positive story about what you learned from the experience.

Here's an example of how he could have given an "honest spin" to his story:

"The truth is, I was not a perfect fit. It wasn't where my passions lie. I wasn't passionate about phones. I am determined to stay on track and pursue a career that fits with my long-term goals and matches up with my strengths so that I can effectively contribute to an outstanding organization. And I have learned that my real passion is [name of the field you are interviewing for]. So I am excited about the tomorrows and know that my last situation was a blessing—it was a positive and I can build from it."

What is your career plan?

Where do you see yourself in five years?

What are your goals in life?

> **The real question:** What commitment do you have to this field? Are your goals aggressive yet realistic?
>
> **Strategy:** Answer honestly, but indicate that you are serious about working in this field. Remember, this is just an interview; no one is asking you to sign up for the rest of your life, but no one wants to hire someone who is just "trying it on for size," either. The mistake people often make is an answer that suggests you are just "exploring" or "trying out" different careers. Although most people change jobs (according to the U.S. Department of Labor's Bureau of Labor Statistics, the average American works for three to five different companies during his professional life), you want to convey that you are pursuing this for your career.

Remember, you are your own agent! So as you answer these types of questions, remain aware of the five tools and bring them to life for people. Attempt to continuously demonstrate that you are (or can become) a five-tool player.

Sending and Receiving Intangible Signals

In both advice meetings and formal interviews, you are trying to ensure that the other person likes and respects you enough to help you or hire you, and you are doing this by showing the intangible reasons you are a good hire. No matter which words you choose to represent your skills and experience (your *tangibles*), there are equally important *intangibles* you must demonstrate. How you say something is just as important as what you actually say.

In any conversation, messages are being sent and received outside of the words; the messages you send and your ability to interpret the messages you receive are part of your style. If you want to be sure the other person recognizes your intangibles, you must be able to decode the messages you are sent and remain in control of the messages you send.

Let's focus first on breaking down the signals you are receiving. By doing this first, you will better understand how you can position yourself in meetings and how to make the transition from a conversation to a chance to ask for additional contacts. These contacts will let you move from the advice meeting you are in to the employment interview you seek.

Reading Your Contact's Signals

Reading the signals you are being sent is the key to demonstrating great timing in your meeting. These signals will enable you to bob and weave effectively through the meeting. There are several things you can watch for and think about while you read the signals being sent to you. The following sections give details on each.

The Interviewer's Interpersonal Style

Interpersonal style is a term used to describe how a person relates to others. Interpersonal style is an expression of personality, but is not the same as personality; interpersonal style is the behavior you see, whereas personality is the internal mechanisms that drive this behavior. For example, there are many introverts (a personality term) who have taught themselves to be active and engaging (an interpersonal style); whereas what you see is a friendly and talkative person, you might not recognize that he or she is consciously thinking "I have to be friendly and talkative." By paying attention to the behavior of the person you are meeting, you can gain clues to help you understand what he is thinking (and begin to think yourself about how you want to respond). There are some common ways to understand the interpersonal style of the person you are meeting and begin to make sense of the personality behind this behavior.

One of the first things you probably notice about people is where they enjoy directing their energy. Some people enjoy spending their energy "inward" on ideas; that is, they enjoy thinking about issues or enjoy playing with concepts and possibilities in their minds. Other people enjoy directing their energy "outward" toward people; that is, they enjoy talking about issues or enjoy bouncing concepts and possibilities off of other people.

We usually call people who enjoy thinking through issues on their own more than talking to others about them introverts, but this term doesn't mean they don't like people. It means they are most passionate about ideas! Introverts get energized when they think about issues and have to spend energy when they socialize. Similarly, we call people who enjoy working through issues with other people more than thinking about them on their own extroverts. They are most passionate about people. Extroverts get energized by interacting with other people, and have to spend energy thinking about issues. Everyone leans toward either introversion or extraversion to some degree; people are a mix, in different ways, of both introverted and extroverted behaviors. If, at the end of a long and tiring week, you can't wait to curl up with a glass of wine and a good book, you might lean toward introversion. If you can't wait to get a beer with your friends, you might lean toward extroversion.

During your meeting, ask yourself "Where does this person probably fall on a scale of introversion and extroversion? Where does she lean?" The answer to this question will help you know on what level you have to "pitch" yourself. With those who lean toward being extroverted, first put more effort into connecting with them personally about your hopes, your goals, and your interests, and then begin to connect about your ideas and plans. With those who lean toward being introverted, put more effort into conveying the rationale of your ideas, your thoughts, and your plans. In other words, try first to connect with them intellectually, and then begin to talk more about personal issues. This doesn't mean one (intellectual or social) is more important than the other—you must connect on both levels. But by understanding even a little bit about your contact's personality by reading their behavior, you can know where to start.

How's It Going?

In every meeting, you must watch for important signals you will be sent about how the meeting is going, and (more importantly) about how the relationship is developing. These signals usually take the form of a "change"—for example, from listening to asking questions, from talking rapidly to talking slowly, or from leaning backward to leaning forward. Being able to sense a change in your contact's style—and to decode the message—is a very important skill to develop. It will help you not only in interviews, but also in all aspects of dealing with people. You could spend years studying all the ways people communicate about their relationships, but here are some very easy signals to watch for.

First, take note of your immediate sense of your contact at the time the meeting started. Was he in a hurry or relaxed? Was she giving you her full attention or distracted? Was the tone of his voice relaxed or urgent? These first notes you are making are to take a baseline reading so that you can notice changes. Now, as the meeting progresses, pay attention to any changes in your contact's behavior because they will signal a change in his thoughts or emotions. For example, if you notice that the pace of his questions is increasing, you might conclude he wants more information. So focus on giving short, precise answers. On the other hand, if you notice she has slowed the pace of questions, you might conclude she is finding less and less in your conversation she wants to know more about. So focus on expanding your answers to give more opportunities to connect.

Also pay attention to the tone of the meeting; changes here are also important. If the tone of the meeting changes from engagement to casual interest, you must recognize this and bring the meeting back to where you want it to be. If you have prepared yourself well and shown your passion, you should find the tone will go from casual interest to full engagement (which is also worth recognizing)!

How to Gather Data

When I sit with a player to talk about "branding" him, I talk about getting him recognition and building a positive image. To do this well, I have to understand the needs and interests of my player and I must position myself as able to respond to these needs and interests. This is key: I can't position myself or our firm as able to help him reach his goals unless I first understand what his goals are. I first must listen and attempt to understand who he is or what his hot buttons are. I can't come out of the gate telling an 18-year-old rookie to wear a business suit everywhere he goes because I want to position him for a J.P. Morgan endorsement. I have to listen first so that I understand what's important to him. He might say the image that is most important to him that he convey is "blue jeans and bubble gum"; knowing this, I know I have to align him with all-American brands such as Chevrolet, not an elite brand like Rolls-Royce. If I had not listened to him, I might have positioned myself incorrectly. It's always better to gather data and then position yourself, versus positioning yourself and then gathering data.

I know, you're thinking "how obvious!" But you would be surprised by how many people I see coming into an interview with *their* agenda in hand and forgetting that the meeting is an opportunity to learn as well as to sell themselves. I've sat in interviews with many potential employees at Career Sports who positioned themselves long before they gathered any data. They come in trying to show me their expertise. It's true I want to understand their skills, but I'm usually not expecting a young adult to be an expert. I want to discover whether they are someone I believe could become an expert. It's all about balance. And staying balanced—bobbing and weaving—means accurately reading the signals of how the meeting is going and responding in ways that create opportunities for you.

Here are some of the best ways to gather important data in a meeting:

- **Listen.** Stop talking and start really listening to what the person is saying—and not saying. Although you have done your research and already have some data, listen well so that you can continue to learn what's important to your contact.

- **Ask great questions.** Ask open-ended questions that could provide compelling answers with data you can use to better position yourself.

- **Look at the items in his office.** Is there a picture of a scene (such as a golf course) that could help you understand things that are important to him? Is there an award from something he has achieved? Ask questions about some of the things that you see that seem important to him; it's a great way to learn more about him.

- **Watch the way she communicates with other employees.** How is she received by other employees? It's important to see whether she is respected by others in the office and is respectful in return. Maybe she takes a phone call while she is with you. How does she treat the person on the other end? These examples can be indications as to whether she will be a good agent for you.

Controlling the Signals You Send

Because the person you are meeting is also trying to read the signals you send, you should be cognizant of your tone and your pace as well. Managing the meeting effectively and asking great questions is one of the first ways you will start to build credibility with your contact. But you must also be aware of the more intangible signals that you are sending through your style—your actions and your body language.

Sending Signals Through Overt Actions

Signals are sent in all kinds of ways. There is a story (who knows whether it's true) that floats around Atlanta, home of the corporate headquarters for the Coca-Cola Company. A businessman was being considered for a very senior role within the Coca-Cola Company and had progressed to the stage of having an interview over dinner with a key Coca-Cola executive. When the waiter arrived to take orders, the candidate spoke before thinking and asked for Diet Pepsi. As the story goes, this was the immediate end of the dinner, the interview process, and the career opportunity. Common sense might tell you that ordering a Pepsi when dining with a Coke executive was a mistake, but there is a bit more to it than just the mistake in behavior.

Those of us who have been to business meetings in the Coca-Cola headquarters building or have been interviewed for a position by them know that they always offer you a drink of one of their products at the start of the meeting. This is more than Southern hospitality; they believe taking the time for a Coke (or a Dasani water, or a Sprite, or any of their other products) truly is "the pause that refreshes" (their original marketing slogan). It would not have taken much thought—or research—to anticipate that it would be smart to order a Coca-Cola if given the opportunity. Doing so (or more to the point, *not* doing so) would be a very basic signal about your understanding of the company. More than the mistake in behavior, it was a mistake of insight and of understanding. This is a blatant example of the truth that wherever you are interviewing, you must act as an extension of that organization's brand, even in the interview.

Let me tell you another story. A young man was in an interview for a sales job. Midway through the meeting, the employer looked at the young man and politely reminded him that "you should never chew gum at a meeting and certainly never on a sales call." The young man calmly looked down, swallowed his gum, looked up with a respectful smile, and said, "What gum?" This gutsy move was exactly the right response for his audience.

Sending Signals Through Body Language

Your body language is another set of signals your contact will be reading. Some of your body language is voluntary (under your control) and some is involuntary (not under your control). But with practice, you can bring the involuntary more under your control.

People tend to interpret some behaviors as signals of comfort and confidence, which in turn create positive impressions. You want to learn to project these signals in order to help wow your contact. People also send signals of anxiety and uncertainty, which in turn create negative impressions. You want to downplay these signals so that you can keep from doing them.

Controlling your body language is not difficult, but you have to think about it. So be careful which signals you send. For example, communication experts say that when people cross their arms in front of their chests, it is a signal of feeling defensive. If you find yourself crossing your arms in front of your chest, uncross them and place them comfortably at your sides. By staying aware of the signals you send, you can make sure you present yourself in a positive, open, and friendly way.

Avoid sending negative signals such as these:

- Blank expression
- Folded arms high on chest
- Leaning backward in the chair
- Excessive looking at hands, shoes, or objects in the office
- Biting your nails
- Touching your face

With practice and conscious thought, you can make the following positive signals voluntary:

- Smiling
- Good posture
- Firm handshake
- Good eye contact
- Nodding head when listening
- Sitting forward on the chair
- Facing toward your contact
- Folding hands together

Attributes of a Successful Candidate

When I interview, I am paying attention to many things outside the skills and other "tangibles" of the candidate. I'm sure other people do the same thing, so you can advance your candidacy by conveying what I think are the five key attributes:

- **Engagement:** Sit on the edge of your seat. Sit up straight. Make eye contact.

- **Interest:** Ask questions. Use the research you've done on the company and your interviewer. Listen carefully and build off the flow of the conversation.

- **Passion:** Show energy and enthusiasm.

- **Respect:** Don't interrupt or imply that what you have to say is more important than listening. Be patient and pick the right opportunities to make your points.

- **Integrity:** Be honest. Don't be "slick" or practiced.

- **Professionalism:** Maintain your energy level. Avoid letting down your guard and acting overly casual. Remember, this is a business meeting in which you are trying to sell your best product (yourself) to your biggest client (your future employer).

Closing the Interview

As the interview winds down, you will come to a point where your interviewer thanks you for your time and interest in the position. At this point, you will need to make a gutsy move. Look your interviewer in the eye, and in a respectful tone, ask something like the following:

> "What do you think are someone's most important assets in order to be successful in this position?"

If he answers this question and notes strengths that match up with what you believe your strengths to be, great. You could follow up with a more detailed question such as these:

> "Do you think my skills and attributes match up with what it takes to be successful in this position and successful inside this company?"

> "Do you have any advice for me?"

Of course, there is a wrong way to ask these questions. The following are wrong because they are not respectful, creative, or unique:

- "How did I do?"

- "So, are you going to hire me?"

- "Do you think I can do this job?"

When you ask a direct question such as "Will I get this job?" you are likely to get a noncommittal answer, even after the best of interviews. It's very rare that positions are given out "on the spot" and without the involvement of many people in the final decision. But by asking some good questions, you can learn what you did well and what you did poorly. Not only do such questions signal that you are coachable, the answers you get to them provide valuable and important information for future situations. And on a more subtle level, you show your contact that you have some guts and aren't afraid to have someone look you in the eye and tell you some good and some bad news. You send a strong message that you are comfortable with feedback and are a person who can be dealt with directly—which are positive qualities in almost any career.

Wrapping Up and Moving On

You've survived your first interview and gained valuable insights. It's time to move forward with the relationships you've built and learn to leverage them most effectively.

CHAPTER 14

Leveraging Your Relationships

Fulfilling your career ambitions is a marathon, not a sprint. And you must be able to finish the race. You are only halfway there once you walk out the door after an interview or advice meeting. Leveraging the relationship after you leave is imperative. Potential employers will be influenced and continually impressed not only by what you did, but what you continue to do—that is, by how effectively you prove the passion that you conveyed in your meeting.

This chapter gives you a look at what goes on in your contact's mind after the interview or meeting. Then it shows what you need to do to further the good impression you made in the meeting and put your contact to work for you.

What Happens After the Interview

Immediately after an interview or an advice meeting, your contact will form judgments based on how well you handled the meeting. If a colleague walked into his office just after you left and asked "Who was that?" would he be more likely to say "That was a really sharp and creative woman who found a way to get in here to meet with me, and who wants to work in this field" or "That was a young woman who begged to get in front of me but really doesn't get it"?

Do you know the most common things we talk about at Career Sports & Entertainment after a candidate finishes an interview? We usually review technical qualifications (that is, the tangibles) first. But, quite frankly, we spend only a few minutes on this because we have screened people in or out of the interview process based on their tangibles long before investing the time to meet with them. Remember that tangibles are used most often as prescreening tools. That is, we choose to meet only the people we know have the tangible qualifications and use the interview to focus on more intangible qualities.

After the tangibles, we talk about whether he "gets it." And this is a major focus for us. We ask ourselves, "Does he have the energy, drive, and persistence it takes to do our work? Is her style one that excites us? Does he share our passion?" Our immediate reactions to this question are indicative of our level of interest in the candidate.

How to Use Follow-Up to Get Others to Be Your Agent

We also notice what happens after the candidate has left our offices. We notice who sends a handwritten follow-up note and how quickly we receive it. Now that your meeting is over, you want to stay in your interviewer's mind, and you want to continue to earn her respect. It's your job to sustain her enthusiasm for you over time. Staying in contact helps you develop someone on the inside to sell you. Up to this point, you have been your own agent, but now you can develop an inside agent, as well.

Remember Matt (see chapter 5), who impressed me with his passionate style, his fearlessness, and his knowledge of public relations? During his interview, I asked him a few specific evidence-based questions about how he would handle securing public relations for several of our clients. He communicated a few ideas about his approach, and I was impressed with his thinking as he was put on the spot. But what wowed me was the e-mail I received a few hours after he left our office.

> *Molly—it was a pleasure meeting you today and learning more about your goals for the Client Rep public relations division. I have put some thought to your questions, and how to secure PR for a few of your guys, and have highlighted a top-line plan below. You will notice it includes an overall objective along with detailed action steps. Would love to get your initial reactions. Again, thank you. I will be in touch later this week. Cheers, Matt.*

Why did this impress me? I was impressed because Matt acted quickly. He provided a great top-line plan that was relevant to my questions even though I didn't ask him to. He sent an e-mail the same day as our meeting, showing me his sense of urgency and the priority he gave to our meeting. He clearly showed me that he listened to, understood, and thought about our conversation. By providing me with a real-time "case study"—without being asked—he showed me that he is proactive, thorough, and insightful.

This e-mail also gave me an opportunity to see his professional approach to our needs. It showed me that he had some guts because he was willing to go out on a limb and provide concrete ideas and opinions. Most important, he showed me that he used the interview as an opportunity to understand what we were looking for and then showed us how he fit the bill.

After each meeting, whether it's an interview or an advice meeting, it's your responsibility to advance the runners, move the ball down the field, take the inside line, or drive to the hoop—you can use any sports analogy you want as long as you recognize that it is up to *you* to further develop the relationship. You must continue to create good, intelligent reasons to remain in touch. Just as it takes several meetings to feel that a person is an acquaintance and then a friend, it takes several touch points for one of your contacts to become comfortable with helping you or hiring you.

Between Matt's demonstration of his passionate style, his intellect in the interview, and his fearlessness in his follow up e-mail, I had a quick sense of what working with Matt would be like before we ever extended him an offer. And we felt we knew Matt better than all of the other people who sent resumes and cover letters.

Have a Post-Meeting Plan

In your follow-up, your minimum goal should be to stay on your contact's radar screen. Ideally, you want to be in the center of it. But remember, your contact has much bigger responsibilities than helping you. Nonetheless, you should steadily build a framework for expanding your relationship.

Here is a simple post-meeting plan to follow:

1. The very first thing you must do when you walk out of a meeting with a contact, whether it was an interview or an advice meeting, is to write down your follow-up timeline and action steps. Do this whether you have agreed to do something (such as send a sample of your work or make a follow-up phone call) or are just thinking through the next steps you want to take to build the relationship. The important thing is to do it now! The specific details and sense of urgency you feel as you come out of the interview will fade across time no matter how clear and obvious they seem to you in that moment. So capture the data you gathered right away:

- Write down notes on any important personal and professional data you gathered from listening (such as spouse's interests, recent projects, professional organizations, and children's names).

- Make notes of any key dates you heard during the meeting, whether they were tied to your contact or the industry as a whole (such as industry events, personal vacations, company-wide meetings, and upcoming professional conferences).

- Make notes of any other information you discovered that is key to understanding your contact's world (any pet peeves he mentioned, his favorite golf course, and so on).

2. Send an e-mail as soon as you get to your computer that begins with a brief thank-you. Also include any specific points that you can pull from the meeting to show that you really listened. Follow up with answers to questions or issues that were left unanswered in the meeting. Close with a second brief thank you. (This is what Matt did so well.)

3. In addition to your immediate e-mail, hand-write a thank-you note and mail it within 24 hours of your meeting. Make sure this note is only a personal thank-you; don't comment on next steps or actions you have agreed to take. Simply thank your contact for her time and attention. Although you responded immediately with an e-mail, sending a hand-written note adds a personal touch.

4. Follow up with any contacts you were given. You should walk out with referrals, and your attentiveness to meeting with them is a clear example of your passion and ability to execute.

This is the process to ensure that you show (through your actions) that you are truly organized, systematic, and committed. By following this process, you will demonstrate your intangibles.

A Sample Follow-Up Timeline

In an effort to recap and effectively demonstrate this process from start to finish, take note of the following sample timeline.

Contact: Steve Kincaid, VP of Dream Careers, Inc.

Date	Action	Next Step
3/1	Secured contact info.	Learn about the contact and company; then try to connect.
3/1	Visited company Web site; reviewed recent article on company in trade journal.	Connect with contact.
3/1	Left voice mail for contact.	Mail letter to contact. Send thank-you e-mail and update note to person who referred me to contact.
3/2	Mailed letter and business card to contact; requested a 15-minute meeting in letter. Sent thank-you note to person who referred me.	Wait five days and call again.
3/7	Second phone call; left voice mail.	Wait five days and call again.
3/10	Contact returned call; secured meeting for 3/20.	Send thank-you card to contact. Send e-mail to referral of contact letting them know I have a meeting set for 3/20.
3/11	Sent thank-you card to contact. Sent update to referral of contact.	Learn more about the contact and the company.
3/12–20	Further gathered information by Googling contact and company and reading all recent issues of relevant trade journals at library. Pulled together the questions to ask contact and	Attend meeting.

(continued)

(continued)

Date	Action	Next Step
	gathered thoughts on answers to questions I might be asked.	
3/20 (a.m.)	Attended meeting.	Send thank-you letter and e-mail to contact; send a thank-you e-mail to referral of contact.
3/20 (p.m.)	Sent thank-you letters and made calls.	Call new contacts gained from meeting. Follow up with current contact in five days.
3/21	Called contacts gained from the meeting.	Start process all over. Continue to follow up with an original contact.

You must also follow up in an effective and timely manner—especially in the way promised and with any actions you have agreed to in your meeting. Inevitably you will walk out of many meetings rejuvenated about your passion. In that moment, you will be motivated to retain and foster the relationship. It's imperative that you retain that motivation day after day because the true test of your relationship-building skills will be how the relationship develops over time.

So, for example, your follow-up strategy might have 10 potential action items. These will be different actions for every meeting you have. In one, you might want to follow up after an industry event where you learned your contact is giving a speech. In another you might want to send an article you read that your contact expressed interest in seeing.

Some will be time-sensitive items whereas others will not be. For example, time- or date-sensitive items might be a key meeting, vacation, speech, or event. You'll need to drop date-sensitive action items into the timeline on the relevant date. You can put non-time-sensitive items in the "notes" section of the person's information in your contact database.

Some potential action items will be things that you won't know well in advance because they simply occur (for example, reading something in a trade publication or a press release, the sale of a company, or the gain or loss of a piece of business). These can be opportunities to communicate something at some level to your contact (congratulations, making them aware that you are aware) so as to let them know you were attentive and listening when you were there and that you are a 24/7 person with your career goals constantly top of mind.

This follow-up process will not only help you track your action steps but also efficiently and effectively track the relationship.

Tracking Your Relationships

As you build a network of great contacts, think of yourself as building a pyramid—a storehouse of opportunities for yourself. Just as in building a pyramid, you will need many, many more contacts as you start at the bottom in order to find the one that tops your network and points up to your dream career.

As you can see, you will be in contact with many more people through my strategy than you would be in a typical job search. Because you will have multiple people you are trying to contact simultaneously, you will need to be more prepared. So you must create a system to manage your network of contacts effectively. The fewer surprises you encounter, the more impressive you will be, and the greater your impact. If you are being aggressive and persistent, you will have an ever-multiplying pool of contacts and many people helping you. You must have a way to remain organized while also being proactive. Meanwhile, each contact needs to feel appreciated enough to sincerely embrace helping you.

You have to be organized to pull this off. You must manage the process and all its details. Create a chart or spreadsheet to help you track your contact with people and make sure you stay on top of what you need to do next. This could look something like the one in figure 14.1.

Name/Contact Information	Company	Referral	Next Steps	Hot Buttons	Status
Steve Kincaid (123) 456-7890 sbk@dreamcareers.com	Dream Careers, Inc.	Jim West	Meeting 3/20	Loves live music	Prep for meeting
John Smith (123) 789-4560	ABC Corp.	Tommy Jones	Meeting 3/21	Widget aficionado	Prep for meeting
Mary West (555) 555-1212	Number One Chick, Inc.	Steve Kincaid	Meeting 3/27	Loves hunting	Send handwritten note to Mary

Figure 14.1: Sample contact spreadsheet.

Build this chart as you gather contacts and begin to secure interviews and advice meetings. Using a system like this is one of the differences between being good and being good enough to secure a great job. Build it, update it, use it, and execute against it.

Wrapping Up and Moving On

You've followed up after your meetings and kept track of your growing list of referrals. It's time to learn how to manage your choices, troubleshoot your search, and reel in the big fish.

Tool Five:
Managing Choices

CHAPTER 15

What to Do When Things Go Wrong

Even though you have a plan for your career search and you're working to execute it flawlessly, things won't always go just as you planned. Maybe you made a slip in one of your interviews, maybe you didn't get the full story about a job in your research, or maybe you have run into a brick wall. This chapter lays out some of the possible worst-case scenarios and helps you make a quick recovery.

Shaq Slips Up

Lenny Wilkens, one of our clients, is one of the few people in the world to be elected into the Basketball Hall of Fame (a.k.a. The Naismith Memorial Basketball Hall of Fame) as both a player and a coach. Lenny was a player from 1960 to 1969 and a player-coach from 1969 to 1975, and became a full-time coach in 1975. As of this writing he is still the winningest coach in NBA history.

In 1994, Lenny was the head coach for the East in the NBA All-Star Game. The NBA All-Star game is once a year, mid-season, when all of the top NBA superstars compete with and against each other. Many of the players on this team weren't born at the start of Lenny's playing career and were most likely in diapers at the onset of Lenny's coaching career.

One of the many stars on the All-Star team was Shaquille O'Neal. Lenny told me this story about an exchange he had with Shaq that is analogous to you as you pursue your dream job: During one of their early workouts, Lenny was running the players through various on-court drills. While he was watching Shaq practice his drop-step to the basket, Lenny walked over to Shaq with a ball and demonstrated, in his typical respectful and classy style, how he would recommend Shaq approach his drop-step. He showed him once or twice, and then they talked about it. Following the exchange, Shaq looked at Lenny and asked, "Did you ever play at this level?" One of the other players heard Shaq's question and pulled him aside and explained that Lenny had indeed played at "this level."

That same afternoon Shaq was talking to his father on the phone. Shaq told him what had happened at practice with Lenny. His father paused and said "Shaq, do you know who Lenny Wilkins is? He is in the Hall of Fame as a basketball player. And he's in the Hall of Fame as a coach, as well. He can teach you a little something about a drop-step."

Later that night in the locker room, Shaq approached Lenny and said, "Hey Coach, I'm sorry about my comments earlier. I told my dad what I said to you, and he told me all about you. You are the man." With that, Shaq pulled out a camera and asked, "Can I get my picture with you, Coach?"

Shaq recovered from the disrespectful comment he made to Lenny because he circled back with Lenny to correct his mistake. He recognized who Lenny was and is, and demonstrated the respect a Hall of Fame player and coach deserves. Shaq wasn't afraid to communicate that he knew about his hiccup, and then used the request for a photo as an additional way to recover and demonstrate his sincere respect for Coach Wilkens. Lenny chuckled as he shared with me the part of the story about Shaq speaking with his father and then Shaq's request for a picture. The relationship was intact. If Shaq had not made this effort, who knows what the status of their relationship might have been? As it was, Lenny was forgiving and chalked it up as the honest mistake of a youthful superstar.

Common Challenges and Solutions

During your advice meetings and your interviews, challenges might present themselves. You might stumble over your words; you might be too direct at times or not direct enough. You might feel one of your answers was not as crisp or as informative as you would have liked. Sometimes these hiccups are deal breakers, but usually you can turn them into just small speed bumps. Shaq turned a potential problem into an honest mistake by the sincerity of his apology and his sense of humor in arriving with a camera.

Hopefully, you will never have to make an apology like Shaq's. But you probably will make some smaller mistakes. Below are some of the most common challenges I see young adults make and my suggested solutions for getting back on track toward a dream opportunity.

Problem #1: You Say Something Stupid

What Could Go Wrong: You say something during a meeting that is insensitive, stupid, or rude.

For example, I was at a final interview with a young woman who Career Sports & Entertainment was very close to hiring as a public relations coordinator. Our entire team was in the meeting and continuing to gain respect for her and collectively seeing her as a potential hire. Toward the end of the interview, I asked, "Do you have any questions for me?" She replied, "Well, yes, one question: As I grow and develop, if I want to move on to another company or agency, will you be helpful to me in that process?" Whoops! She had just blown it by implying that she was prepared to use us as a stepping-stone and also suggesting she would outgrow us.

This was a bad question to ask someone like me who had invested 12 years into growing CS&E and growing *with* the company. It was a bad question to ask someone whose focus is on creating tremendous stability in our company. And it was a really bad question to ask someone who was trying to decide whether or not to hire her and put her in a position to be in direct contact with our clients. The last thing I want to do is have someone building relationships in and outside of our agency who is not committed to being with us for the long term.

Why It Could Go Wrong: You lack awareness of and have not researched the world of your contact or interviewer (both her personal and professional worlds).

Our example candidate wasn't intuitive enough to understand the dynamics of the situation. She should have clearly gathered from her first interview, her visits to our office, and the majority of her second interview that we had long-term employees and that we have fostered a special family environment.

How to Fix It: Immediately address your slip. If you asked a question or made a statement that was insensitive or disrespectful, acknowledge it, "spin it" with a clever comment, or simply apologize for it. And handle it in the moment if you can, or at your first opportunity after the meeting. It is probably not hard for you to think of examples where the handling of a problem was worse than the problem itself—whether in politics, your friendships, or your own life. Relationships are challenging, and can sometimes end in a "car wreck." In both traffic accidents and relationships, we are often most offended not by the actions but by what we assume the other person's intentions to be: "You were driving like a maniac! You have no self-control!" When you can show your intentions were not to create a problem, and that you are willing to immediately take steps to repair any damage that might be done, most people will respond favorably to you.

Upon realizing she asked a bad question, our example candidate could have said in a sincere tone, "Molly, I respect this company greatly. Candidly, I am in an environment now that is openly a short-term situation for everyone—six months to a year. However, I do believe the opportunity you are offering me will be a long-term move for me. I see how special this environment is. I am smarter and more intuitive than my question would demonstrate. Is there anything else I can do to prove to you and your team that I am capable of committing for the long term?"

Once you have sincerely addressed your slip, move on. The truth is, you might not be able to completely repair the relationship. But unless you address it quickly and openly, you definitely will not begin to repair it. If you fail to properly address your mistake by the end of the meeting, but later reflect on the meeting and realize it was a mistake, you can follow up with an e-mail or phone call very soon after the meeting as well. Here's an example of what our example candidate could have said in this situation:

> *Molly, as I am reflecting back on our meeting, I want to make sure you know I didn't intend to imply that CS&E couldn't be a long-term home for me. I should have explained in our meeting my existing environment; we very openly discuss how the company can support us as we move up and move out. From day one here, everyone was aware I would be moving on from my role within a year. I know your environment isn't that way, and I love and respect that. My question was a mistake and very much a result of my current environment. I am smarter and more intuitive than that question would demonstrate. I hope you can trust this follow-up and know that I am intensely intrigued and eager to have the opportunity to permanently join your team.*

If she had either called or e-mailed something like this with sincerity and honesty, she might have reopened the door with us. But the door was definitely closed when she failed to acknowledge and address the situation.

Problem #2: You're Not Qualified for the Job

What Could Go Wrong: During the meeting, you realize you aren't as qualified for the job as you, your contact, or your interviewer had expected. But you love the company and the people in it and are still interested.

Why It Could Go Wrong: You failed to research the position well enough, or the employer failed to report the position to you accurately.

How to Fix It: This challenge has a couple of different scenarios and a couple different solutions.

This issue could surface in several different ways. First, the person you are interviewing with might realize that you are underqualified for the position and address it openly. Second, you might read his signals and based on his tone and comments determine he has some concerns about your lack of qualifications. Third, you might realize you are not aligned on the role as the person you are meeting with begins to share information with you about the position but before you have shared much information about yourself.

If the interviewer openly addresses her concern or you are simply picking up on her concerns, I suggest you talk openly about the benefits of hiring a "virgin in the field." You won't have any bad habits to break like she might have to do with a more veteran businessperson, and you are ready to learn things her way from the start.

If you realize that you might be underqualified before the interviewer has had an opportunity to realize it, I suggest you ask more questions before you divulge too much about your concerns. Ask "Are you interested in training someone your way?" "Are you interested in having someone be pretty moldable?" "Do you want a more veteran-type hire?"

If you get back answers like, "I don't want to have to break a lot of bad habits" or "I want a young, coachable person that I can teach my way of doing things," then great. You can openly address that that is who you are. But if you get answers like, "I need someone who is ready to go" or "I want someone who needs very little guidance and teaching because I just don't have the time to teach" then great. Be direct about the fact that you might not be the perfect fit but yet you value his relationship and would welcome his advice on the next steps to become ready or, if that isn't likely to happen, other great people that the person you are meeting with knows and might be more appropriate for you to get in front of.

Problem #3: You Realize You Don't Like the Interviewer or the Company

What Could Go Wrong: You have an interview and learn you don't like the company, its products, or its people or you don't like the person you are meeting with and don't want her to "be your agent" in your job search.

Why It Could Go Wrong: If you don't like the company, you probably didn't do enough research. It's very hard to know in advance whether you will like the people, although you will have a good sense during your meeting. Perhaps your contact says something insulting or inappropriate or does something that offends you. You get a gut feeling that they aren't good people, or you hear stories while there that feel inconsistent with your value system.

How to Fix It: Although this company isn't a fit for you, remember that your interviewer still could help get you in front of other people. So, unless you believe a link with this contact would clearly be a negative for you, use the contact to learn and build relationships outside this company. After the interview, send her a pleasant handwritten note thanking her for her time. But make a note on your spreadsheet that "this is not someone I want representing me—no need to recruit further."

Problem #4: A Prior Problem Comes Back to Haunt You

What Could Go Wrong: You learn there is someone that you have a poor personal relationship with already working in the organization.

Why It Could Go Wrong: Because you have studied for and already built many contacts in this field, you're likely to find previous acquaintances working at some of your target companies.

How to Fix It: Carefully assess how closely you will be working with the person you don't like. Will you cross paths as colleagues or work closely together on a daily basis, or is this a fairly large company and you could never see each other nor work together? To gather data so that you can better assess your future working relationship with the other person, you could ask your contact the following questions that do not immediately reveal your concerns:

- It was nice to see Fred. Would I be working closely with Fred Flintstone?

- Although we didn't see Fred today, just curious: Would I work for Fred Flintstone?

- As you might know, Fred and I grew up together. Would I have any interaction with Fred Flintstone?

If you would work closely together, it's my advice to address the issue from a professional standpoint. Address it first with the individual you have a conflict with and then, if necessary, with the individual doing the hiring. You might be able to come to a positive resolution with the individual and not need to address it at a higher level. Should you need to address it with the person making the hiring decisions, pinpoint the challenge with the employer in a short and professional manner and marry the introduction of the challenge with your solution. Be honest and sincere about the situation (how you feel) without compromising the privacy of the other person—that is, you can talk about your discomfort and the strain in the relationship without discussing the details of why you have a strained relationship. Avoid laying blame; remember that you have not been hired yet, but your rival has. Be prepared to outline your plan for improving the relationship.

You need to be aware that the individual you have an issue with might try to box you out of the opportunity. I would still suggest addressing it with the person. The truth is, it's always healthy to address a problem directly and take that risk. You don't need to walk in on day one with issues or interpersonal challenges. You might also ask to speak "off the record" with the interviewer, and share that you have had disagreements with Fred Flintstone in the past and are concerned he could prevent your skills and fit for the position from being evaluated objectively. Usually, raising this concern is enough to ensure a potential employer will work to make a fair decision, but the reality is that they will not likely make a move that could increase the potential for problems in their organizational culture. Although you can try to overcome this barrier, it may be best to look elsewhere.

If you assess the situation and you could very likely never cross paths because it is a nationwide company, with multiple offices and thousands of employees, addressing it might not be necessary because the situation is irrelevant professionally.

Problem #5: You Hit a Brick Wall

What Could Go Wrong: You encounter a contact who very firmly says he really doesn't think he can help you at all, although you believe he can.

Why It Could Go Wrong: Your contact might not *want* to help. Your contact might honestly not see how he can help you. Or your contact might be testing your passion, your intensity, and your follow-up.

How to Fix It: After the meeting, update your spreadsheet with your data from the meeting and your next action steps. Do a few creative things following the meeting to recruit this agent further. For example, if he is leaving three days later for a bike trip in Italy, e-mail him the morning of his trip simply wishing him a wonderful and safe trip to Italy. Or, if he told you that this weekend he will be hosting his daughter's birthday party, e-mail on Friday and wish him a wonderful birthday celebration with his daughter.

If you get tremendous pushback or a complete lack of follow-up from him after multiple e-mails or calls, move on. You tried and he doesn't want to help you. If you have followed up and he is becoming more responsive, continue to build the relationship by remaining consistently, uniquely, and respectfully persistent. Busy people are willing to help only the people who are energetic enough to want to help themselves. Show him—through your follow-up—that your passion in that meeting was real.

Problem #6: You Don't Want the Job the Interviewer Thinks Is Right for You

What Could Go Wrong: You go in for an informational meeting or interview about one job and your contact starts accelerating you toward a different job that you don't want. For example, you come in to interview for a marketing or sales type position but they indicate that you aren't ready—they only hire people with at least one year of experience and advise to you to consider a receptionist or office manager role for a year and "see how it goes."

Why It Could Go Wrong: You have not conveyed your true passion or level of skill. You have not sold them on your capabilities.

How to Fix It: Address your objections to taking the position honestly but respectfully. Re-communicate your vision, your passion, your experiences, and your skill sets. Respectfully help her understand that you would only divert this drastically from your immediate vision if you could better understand how taking a position like this position isn't a liability but an asset for you.

Share that your gut tells you that you would be viewed by clients and employees in a different light in this type of role; but if people have taken a receptionist role in the past and it catapulted them into a position like you are seeking that it could be interesting. Be intensely sensitive and respectful in your delivery so as not to come off in an arrogant or presumptions manner.

If she doesn't seem to be able to articulate that this is a great stepping stone, show appreciation for her effort to help you—even if it is misdirected.

You might say something like this:

> *I appreciate your efforts in trying to fit me into this fantastic company. It seems like such a special organization. But I don't know that the particular opportunity you're presenting matches up with my long-term goals. I know you try to find people who can be a perfect fit for the long term. As I mentioned, my passion is really to be [name of position you're seeking], not [name of position the other person sees you in]. Maybe one day I'll regret this conversation, but for right now, it's what my heart tells me. I don't want to look back in life and say "what if"—I want to pursue my dream career right now.*

The other person will respect you for being honest and steadfast in your goals. And you'll avoid being railroaded into something you don't want to do.

Problem #7: Your Contact Intimidates You

What Could Go Wrong: You feel intimidated by a referral your contact gave you and are reluctant to reach out and meet with him.

Why It Could Go Wrong: You lack enough self-confidence; the contact is important enough that if you blow the meeting, it could hurt you.

How to Fix It: You must over-prepare (and you must get over it!) You can overcome your fear by doing extensive research about your referral and his company. Learn as much as you can about the referral so that you have plenty of data you can draw on during the meeting. Have your stories or nuggets in your pocket ready to use. Try acting "as if" this contact is one of your oldest friends, and talk to him in the same comfortable manner. Additionally, be cognizant of the messages you are sending yourself and send yourself the right messages, as discussed in chapter 7.

Problem #8: You Don't Respect the Person Your Contact Refers You To

What Could Go Wrong: Your contact provides you with a referral to a company or a person you don't respect.

Why It Could Go Wrong: Your contact might not share your same morals or might not have the same viewpoint on the person or company you object to.

How to Fix It: Determine the root cause for your lack of respect. Is it that the company (or the contact provided) stands for issues that are inconsistent with your own values? If so, send a thank-you note to the contact who referred you and note in your spreadsheet about the referral you were given that "this is not my kind of company—no need to pursue." But keep in mind, for your contact to respect you, you must make him aware of your reasoning for not following up with his referral. Just be honest.

I greatly respect the idea of staying true to your beliefs and your values, but consider something. Unless your contact displayed something that made you question *his* character, give him the benefit of the doubt. You do not know who else he might be able to refer you to. For example, just because a contact refers you to another contact working for an alcohol distributor (and you object to drinking) doesn't mean that first contact doesn't know more good, relevant people who could help you. So it might make sense to continue to build the relationship so that the contact likes and respects you enough to want to help you further.

Wrapping Up and Moving On

You've learned how to recover from several possible problems. It's time to close the deal.

CHAPTER 16

Closing the Deal

If you use the tools I've introduced and discussed in the preceding chapters, you will create choices for yourself—several different job options. Having choices allows you to work toward your goals. Having choices gives you a sense of control and minimizes the paralyzing sense of vulnerability or insecurity you might feel when you're looking for a job.

At some point after all your hard work, all your networking, all your time-lines, all your e-mails, all your voice mails, and all your phone calls, you will get the offer that starts you toward your own dream career. Notice I said "*starts* you toward your dream career."

The odds are your first job in your target industry will not be the job you want forever. Mine sure wasn't! I answered the phone, saying "Super Bowl Twenty Eight" at least 100 times a day for almost six months, dawn to dusk. Clearly I didn't spend my 16 years of formal education learning to answer phones! I took that job—knowing it would be exactly what it was—because it eventually led me to my current one. I looked at the positives everyday. I embraced the opportunity to build great relationships with some very key executives in Atlanta. I never took my eye off the ball, and as you have tough days doing your first job in your newly chosen career field, remember not to take your eye off the ball either. Stay focused on the long-term goals—stay focused on the positives—and be willing to adapt. Rarely does anyone go directly from college to being the CEO of a major corporation. You aren't going to walk into "heaven" every day, but every day that you grind through it is a stepping stone for greater tomorrows.

This chapter is about managing your choices when you receive a job offer: evaluating it, modifying it, accepting it, or declining it gracefully. And in keeping with the theme of managing your relationships throughout this book, I talk about the important step keeping your contacts informed about which choices you've made.

Receiving and Evaluating an Offer

Let's look at the process of being offered and accepting a job in more depth.

Getting the Call

You will probably receive a verbal offer first, usually in a phone call from your future boss, the human resources representative, or both. When these people tell you the details over the phone, just listen. Listen calmly, listen carefully, and listen politely. No matter what, be appreciative and honored by the offer. Remember, it really is hard to get the tough jobs, and the person at the other end of the line offering you a start truly believes it is your lucky day. She expects you to be excited, and you should be. Don't start this phase of your relationship on a negative note—be excited that an offer has come and show it!

There will be time to review the details before you commit, so be enthusiastic and upbeat during the initial offer (and remember—by showing enthusiasm, you signal that you truly do want to work for this company). When you present concerns later, your potential employer will have already seen your enthusiasm and is more likely to take your concerns seriously. If you have some concerns about the goals and expectations for the position, feel free to ask a few positive and upbeat questions to attempt to understand the opportunity better.

There are four areas you want to have clearly defined:

- What is the work I am being asked to do?

- How will I be expected to get this work done?

- How will you, the employer, assist me in doing this (with training, support, resources)?

- How will I be evaluated and paid?

This can be a very exciting phone call, and it's okay to show that you're excited. However, never accept an offer on the spot. Ask when a written offer will be provided. The written offer will help you understand exactly what you are signing up for. Asking for it also shows that you are a thorough, careful person who does not jump into deals without careful consideration.

What to Say

As great as it is to get the call, there are different ways to handle the situation. Here's an example of a somewhat exaggerated but wrong way to respond to an offer on the phone, followed by a better response.

Wrong:

> Wow, fantastic! I'll take it! I really didn't think I did that great in the interview and wasn't sure what you would do, but now I'm psyched. Just so you know, I can't work 8 to 5, it needs to be more like 9 to 4 and I'll need three weeks off in June.

Right:

> Thank you so much! This is certainly an exciting phone call. I'm so honored! Thank you! Could you e-mail me this offer or send something in writing? I'll review it and get back to you before noon tomorrow. Is that timing okay?

It is important to ask for time to consider the offer because, most likely, as you get past the excitement of receiving the offer, you will have questions. Maybe the salary is less than you had hoped, you will be assigned to a city you hadn't pictured living in, or you will be reporting to someone different than you expected.

Think About What's Important to You

After you have received and reviewed the details of the offer, you need to pull back and determine what is most important to you. From a negotiating standpoint, you need to identify your key "must haves" and begin to move forward to secure them. You also need to think about what you are willing to give up in order to secure this job. You should have a checklist of details that are important and relevant. Remember, it is important to stay unemotional as you review the offer and solidify the details. Make a list of all the areas, such as the following:

- Salary or other compensation plan

- Bonus opportunities

- Review/increase schedule

- Insurance (health, life, dental, disability)

- Vacation

- 401(k) retirement plan (with matching contributions)

- Holidays

- Vacation days

- Sick days

- Educational reimbursement

- Relocation reimbursement

As you hone in on what is most important to you, remember to be realistic and respectful to the organization. Before you start pushing the envelope and asking too much, step back and think about this as if you were the employer. You are someone new to the field with limited or no relevant career experiences. This job is going to be a stepping stone for you, and both you and your employer know it. Often, the company will have an entry-level salary range already defined. So don't take your eye off your long-term goals. It's not always about money and benefits—sometimes it's about the opportunity. Ask yourself questions such as these:

- Do I believe this is a great opportunity?

- Is there real growth potential?

- Will my supervisor "have my back" and embrace my growth?

- Will I build great relationships?

My advice is that if the answer to these questions is "yes" and this is what you are passionate about, don't lose the opportunity by trying to get too much. You might be tempted to try to get a couple of thousand dollars more out of them at the start. Don't do it. I make a living pushing the financial envelope for our clients, and I'm telling you this is *not* the right time for you to do the same. Starting out in a new industry, you really haven't done anything yet. Pushing for an extra $75 every two weeks won't change your life, but it could change your relationship with the organization. Before you get upset with this advice, let me explain.

First evaluate whether your desire to have the offer adjusted stems from ego-driven reasons or necessity-driven reasons. Stay focused on the long term; keep the prize in mind. With that prize in mind, if there are areas that you are unhappy about—that you feel are not fair—use the strategy in the next section to attempt to get them adjusted.

Adjusting an Offer

In a very positive and upbeat tone, make it clear that the offer is very exciting to you but is at a lower salary than you hoped or is in a location that is different than you had hoped. Make it clear that this is disappointing, but that you intend to accept the offer, come on board, and show them exactly what an incredible value you bring. Then, using a low-key, soft-spoken, but direct tone, ask the following important strategic questions:

- If I do exceed your expectations, where would you expect I'll be rolewise and salarywise in one year?

- Is my first review and raise based on a standard percentage increase or is it based more specifically on what I have accomplished?

In most business settings, the answer will be that your one-year raise is subjective within a set range based on the value you bring to the company. What you are attempting to confirm (very respectfully) is that you don't think your compensation package is quite what you wanted but that, after a stellar first year, they will step up to keep a great employee happy. When you accept the position, you send them a clear message that you believe in yourself, that you are confident, and that you will deliver. And, in a small way, you aren't afraid to take a risk. All of these things will make you very attractive to most employers.

Accepting an Offer

When you are comfortable in embracing the opportunity, call and accept the position.

The following is an example of how to do this:

> Hi, I promised to get back to you after reviewing the offer in writing. I want you to know how excited and appreciative I am about this opportunity. I accept, and I can't wait to get started!

Send a follow-up e-mail confirming your acceptance and again stating how excited you are about joining "the family."

Declining an Offer

If you decline the offer, be sure you are appreciative. Your overall tone while declining a job needs to be one that allows the other person to hear your sincere appreciation for his interest in you. Be respectful because your paths might cross down the road and all good relationships are important—so never burn a bridge. Additionally, ensure that you are clear in your reasoning for declining the offer without sounding unsure or apologetic.

The following are some wrong and right examples of how to do this:

Wrong (in an e-mail):

> Hi Steve. Thanks for the offer, but I found something better. It offers more money and stuff. So I won't be taking the lower-level job you offered. Thanks anyway!

Right (over the phone):

> Steve, thank you so much for your time and your effort in putting together this offer. I have really enjoyed learning about your organization. At this point, I am staying focused on my long-term goals, and although it would be a wonderful experience to accept this offer, I have decided to accept an offer with Dream Careers, Inc. It will better direct me toward my primary passions. Again, thank you, and I will stay in touch.

Informing Others Who Helped You

Next it's time to notify and thank all the people who helped you get to this point in your search. Phone calls are more personal, but e-mails are certainly appropriate, too. All of those you have met with along your job search journey should receive one or the other.

First, contact all the people you met with within the company where you are taking the position. Let them know you are taking the job and how excited you are. Thank each of them for providing advice and insight.

Second, do the same for anyone you met with in the advice meetings and interviews that led you to this job offer. You need to notify them that you have accepted the opportunity as well.

Third, contact all the people you went to for advice—whether or not they were "directly" connected to this offer. It is always appreciated to know the outcome of the story when you have taken the time to give someone advice.

The following are example right and wrong e-mails:

Wrong:

> Steve, I got an offer. It's pretty good, not all I wanted, but it's OK. I guess I'm not sure it's the right long-term position for me, but it's the right one for now, so I took it. Thanks for your help!

This is wrong because it minimizes the help offered by this contact. They took action on your behalf and it sounds as though you are not appreciative, or that they did not do enough for you. Also, it sounds as if you are compromising your long-term goals. And it has an overall tone of someone who is lacking confidence and is comfortable with complacency.

Right:

> Molly, I am very excited to tell you that I just accepted a job offer! Your advice was excellent, and I greatly appreciate the introduction to Dr. Kincaid. I was able to meet with Steve last week, and have now been offered a Marketing Coordinator position at Dream Careers, Inc. This is going to allow me to understand sponsorship relevant to properties and corporations in great detail. I can't thank you enough for your insight and encouragement. Your willingness to let me look inside and learn from your own career was so helpful, and your suggestion to talk with Steve turned out to be critical in locating this position. I sincerely appreciate all of your efforts and know this opportunity was due to your support. I plan to stay in touch. Again, thanks so much for your advice.

Be sure you are appreciative and make your contacts feel like they were a part of your success in finding this opportunity. Tell them why you are so excited about this new position without criticizing any other opportunities you didn't take. And don't make any of these calls or send any of these e-mails—taking yourself off the market—until you have definitely been offered and accepted a position.

Don't Hear "No"

Let's talk quickly about learning you have not been selected for a job you really wanted. You have a choice: Hear and accept the "no" or try to influence their decisions. Throughout his career, one of my friends has had four or five candidates that were rejected for a job call him to politely say "You made a mistake." Although these callers might not have landed a job in the end, they usually got a second look. They created another opportunity for themselves to demonstrate their styles and their skill sets. The phone call showed their tenacity and their confidence in their ability to contribute. They didn't hear "no," which in various careers is what it takes to be successful.

If it is a sales job you weren't selected for and you circle back with a phone call saying, "You made a mistake," that might get his attention. And it's even better when you circle back with some real-life tangible examples. Get him to turn his head back toward you again, and do it in an effort to secure another meeting in which you can provide real case studies relevant to their business solutions. Illustrate ideas that prove your ability to be successful in this job—and you might just successfully change his mind. Stay fearless!

Wrapping Up and Moving On

Congratulations! You have now accepted a position with a reputable firm and taken the first step toward your dream career in a field you love. It's been a long journey. You have fearlessly executed your game plan with passionate style and created choices for yourself. And it worked. Now bring these five tools into your career, too!

Welcome to the Big Leagues

You have learned how to embrace the five tools to start yourself toward the career you dreamed about having. You have been your own career agent and created a path that lets you wake up every day knowing you love your work. The wonderful truth is that you can—and must—apply these five tools to every area of your life with equal success. Although this book is aimed at helping you start the path toward your dream career, it wouldn't be complete without a word about what you do after you land your first job in your target career field. How can you ensure success—and the opportunities that success will bring?

In some ways, you are like a child taking her first steps. Those first few efforts might be scary and tough, but once you master working in this career, you will find it opens up a whole new world to you.

Remember, *the tough jobs are tough to get because they aren't easy!* Let me say that in a slightly different way—the tough jobs go to people who are tough enough to get them, tough enough to keep them, and tough enough to excel in them. This career is *your* passion, *your* dream, and *your* life. Set your goals in order to motivate yourself to do the maximum, not to meet the minimum expectations. When challenges arise, remember that tough times don't last, but tough people do!

In many ways, the way to ensure success once you are in your dream job is to continue to use the tools that got you there. Just as these tools separated you from everybody else during your search, they will help you stand out from everybody else in your big-league career. It's no different than how we ensure our clients stand out and capitalize on opportunities as their careers flourish. By following my approach, you will feel like you know your new boss, and he will feel like he knows you. You will already have a wealth of advice and "inside information" from all of your advice meetings and your interviews. Due to your strategic approach to locking up a tough job, your new boss will have a taste of your tenacity. He will recognize that you have the passion for the business, the creativity, and the fearlessness to create choices.

You have all the tools and knowledge you need to build your career. You understand that the road to the desk you are sitting at was tough and competitive, but the tough times were worth it. You recognize that your passionate style, your fearlessness, your game plan, your ability to execute, and your management of the choices that arose brought you here. And you have seen first hand that your ability to get people to like you enough to want to hire you or help you is an important skill set. Now let's translate, at the most basic level, the skills you have learned and implemented to help you grow as a professional.

Implementing the Five Tools on the Job

Initially, you will demonstrate with your actions your daily commitment to the brand of your company, its integrity, and your coworkers. So be there for other employees, support other areas of the company, stay late, and be willing to "pick up the dirty towels." You are collecting a paycheck, so take pride and make an effort to exceed their expectations by applying the five tools to every aspect of your job.

Tool 1: Your Passionate Style

Your *passionate style* is exemplified by how quickly or slowly you walk down the hall. It is exemplified by the energy in your voice when you talk about what you do. You want this career because you love it, not because of money. Most athletes pursued their sport because they love it—they had a passion for it—not because they ever thought they might make $10 million a year on a baseball field. Your passion and style toward your career is exemplified by your thoughts and actions not only at work, but at night and on the weekends—away from the job. You are the kind of person who wants to listen, see, and soak up things around you in your life away from the office that could contribute to your employer's success. Your passionate style is demonstrated by your 24/7 attitude!

Talk about what you do for your employer using the word "we," not the words "I" or "they." Remember, you are part of a team! Show a genuine and sincere concern for the entire company. Be constantly aware that you are part of something bigger. Your job contributes to the overall success or failure of the company, so constantly recognize the importance of pulling back out of your daily tasks to embrace how what you are working on might impact the overall goals of the company.

Ensure that the entire company views you as someone who knows how to work hard and is not afraid to do the dirty work. Improve the company atmosphere with a positive "can-do" business attitude. When your boss asks you to do something, never pause and look up as if to imply that you are questioning the assignment. As the mentor of a friend put it, "Your only real job at this stage is to make your boss look good. Do that, and the rest will follow." Worry about your job description only from the standpoint of what you can over-deliver on each day.

The passionate style that captured your contact in the first two-and-a-half minutes of your initial meeting is the same style that will enable you to capture clients and colleagues. Use your passion to build relationships with your colleagues that would be very difficult to replace, and build relationships externally that cannot be replaced. Whether you are an agent, a salesperson, or an accountant, things always work better when people like you! So get your clients, your boss, your colleagues, the receptionists, the interns, the janitor, and even the competitors you encounter to like and respect you enough that if you needed help, they would provide it.

Your style is your image and your "brand," so be memorable. Smile! And smile often. Always stay calm and stay organized. Be sure your brand represents someone who knows how to behave at various moments in time based on his or her situation.

Your style allows you to build strong and lasting relationships. It helps you position yourself as irreplaceable. Your style is represented by your sense of urgency and your ability to operate under pressure. Your style needs to represent a happy, "glass is half full" type of person. People inherently like to be around happy, healthy, mature people. So make your style contagious!

The following are some key ways to make certain your style shines through:

- Dress with class and professionalism—always.

- Add value daily; bring ideas and opportunities to the forefront constantly.

- Avoid negativity. Avoid participating in gossip about colleagues—it's never healthy. Pick your work "friends" carefully and remain extremely professional; don't let down your guard with people you work with.

- Be respectfully different; be that person that people respect because you are consistently good at what you do.

- Do the little things right. It's the little things that help make you lucky. Become known as the guy who goes the extra mile and brings passion and creativity to all his work.

- Prove you can manage yourself and your time effectively.

- Always, always close the loop with clients and colleagues. Follow up and do it consistently. If someone asks for something, do it quickly and more thoroughly than expected.

- Know your strengths and your weaknesses. Stay focused on improving your weaknesses while building off your strengths.

- Make yourself irreplaceable.

Tool 2: Your Fearlessness

Pursue your personal growth (and in turn, the growth of your company) *fearlessly.* Assert controlled aggressiveness, operate with intensity, and manage your drive for success without alienating your colleagues. In other words, don't sit back timidly and think you will advance in an organization only by executing and implementing the line items in your job description. Add value by being fearless and sharing ideas they might not expect from a rookie. Here are some ways to exemplify your fearlessness:

- **Take calculated risks.** Combine respect with guts. Use your smarts and create moments within an organization where you can go out on a limb and add value. For example, don't be afraid to express your opinion when you've done your research and believe you're right—even if that opinion is different from what others are saying.

- **Take control respectfully and consistently, and without being overbearing.** In my career (and in yours) you have to earn "the ball." And when you get "the ball," take it and "score." For example, we are the quarterback for our clients' careers. We must be in control and remain a consistent advocate for our clients and their families. We earned the right to manage their lives, and it's our responsibility to take control—and to "score." You earned your job; now be the quarterback.

- **Don't hear "no."** People say no when they don't see your value or understand the ways you can have a positive impact on the business. So you will get some "no's"; but remember that it's an opportunity to continue to learn and understand them and their business so you can identify more ways you can add value.

- **Believe in yourself (don't doubt yourself).** In other words, send yourself positive messages that you believe in yourself and your ability to execute. When a golfer stands over a putt to win a tournament, or a pitcher comes in to close out a baseball game, he must send himself the right messages: "I will drain this putt" or "I can throw this slider on a dime and will strike this guy out for the win." Your boss and your clients are more comfortable entrusting themselves to someone who believes in their ability to deliver consistently.

- **Be more aggressive than most, but don't be annoying.** When I begin to have contact with a player, coach, or broadcaster who is considering signing with us, I walk a tightrope. I must be consistently, uniquely, and respectfully aggressive. I want him to know our passion, our game plan for his career, and our ability to execute, but I must pick my spots and read his needs and priorities. As you cut your teeth in your career, remember to walk that tightrope as well so that your clients and coworkers never misinterpret you as being too boisterous. Communicate your opinions and your solutions, but recognize that you can learn from others.

Tool 3: Your Game Plan

You've managed your career search effectively and have gotten a position you want. Now you need to manage your career in the same way. Always keep the big picture in mind—*your long-term game plan*. Anticipate, anticipate, anticipate! Have a plan and a strategy for your next several career moves—not only in your head, but on paper. Every day, stay focused on not only your own game plan but the game plan of the entire company. Share your business growth strategy with select associates and with your boss because it's important for them to know that you have a plan.

Keep your head out of the sand, even on busy days or weeks, and recognize the big picture. Ask your boss everyday, "What more can I do today?" or better yet, offer solutions, concepts, ideas, and information based on what you know is going on.

Try to do all of the following:

- Operate with a future-oriented mentality.

- Be organized and over-prepared for meetings.

- Provide great ideas that support the business strategy.

- Always stay focused on "over-delivery" in an effort to expand your personal role and knowledge base, which in return will support corporate growth.

- Keep your eye on the ball using your game plan; but also follow your heart.

Tool 4: Your Flawless Execution

Strive for perfection in everything, from your internal e-mails to letters to clients. Make sure that you spell names correctly and that your spreadsheets can't have holes poked in them. In many professional environments, lack of flawless execution won't be tolerated. Someone is paying you to do a job. Do it well and do it right. The reputation of the company depends on it and your respect hinges on it. Here are some tips for executing flawlessly:

- **Be detailed and thorough.** For example, be detailed in your e-mails, your letters, and your interpersonal communication. When I reach out to a client, a prospect, or an employee, I ensure that the e-mail or letter contains all the information he needs and has no errors. If it didn't, he might wonder whether I would represent him in the same careless manner. Also be detailed in your listening. Hear your boss's or coworkers' requests and their needs so that you can act on them effectively. A lack of thoroughness or attention to details could get you fired.

- **Be attentive.** Respond within minutes or hours to clients, employees, and all others (regardless of the day of the week). It sends the message that they are a priority and your career is a priority to you as well. When a player calls and needs to talk, I almost always answer my phone (unless I'm at church or in the shower). When they request we have dialogue with a general manager, a network, or an athletic director about a situation, we make that phone call immediately. We tell them they are a priority and our actions must consistently match our promises.

- **Be perceptive of your image and your intangibles.** If you have a big-league job, you have to dress and act like a big-league player. Look professional and act like someone who takes his career very seriously. When we are at a baseball game, we wear our business clothes; when I go to dinner with a client, I dress the way they would want their agent to dress. Additionally, I remain professional—always. As friendly or as close as I am to our clients, it is a business relationship and they respect my consistently professional approach to all situations.

- **Be analytical.** Think things through from start to finish. Process the possible outcomes; process the positives and the negatives of various opportunities. When I embark on a contract negotiation, I understand all angles: the data, the relationships involved, the history of those relationships, the moving parts in the situation, and so on. Remain analytical in all you do in your career. But don't paralyze yourself with your analytics; rather, use them as a tool to better solve problems and see opportunities.

Tool 5: Managing Choices

As your career progresses, you will be faced with many important decisions. Do I fight for a project I think will add value, or do I support my boss who thinks it's a mistake? Do I put more of my time and energy into sales or serving existing clients? Do I move to a smaller office on the West Coast for a bigger role and title? You will create *choices* for yourself to manage by successfully and consistently staying cognizant of the preceding four tools. People are promoted inside companies if they have passion, style, fearlessness, a game plan, and execution. People are successful in and outside organizations when they have these four key ingredients. Once you have mastered the other four tools, you will have growth opportunities. And, as you grow and make choices and develop your skills along various paths, you will grow, both personally and professionally.

Managing your choices wisely will give your new boss respect for you. She will recognize that you have a passion for the business and the ability to think analytically about the issues your business presents.

Surround Yourself with Five-Tool Players

Equally important to mastering these tools is surrounding yourself with other people who share your five-tool approach. These are people you can respect and often learn from. The people you surround yourself with don't have to have the same interests as you. But they must be five-tool players. You must also choose friends (and since you've chosen the right company, colleagues) who have a passionate style, fearlessness, a game plan, and the ability to execute while they create choices for themselves.

Whether it be your friends or your colleagues, spend your time with people who "get it." Five-tool players "get it"; they understand that doing the little things matters. Five-tool players are also people who are constantly trying to improve both personally and professionally. One of the things amateur golfers talk about is that they would rather tee it up with golfers who have a good swing, good rhythm, and a good demeanor on the golf course. They don't want to go play with someone who is going to shoot 80 with a horrible swing and is negative, because often that might impact the amateurs' game. The same is true in life and in business. So, tee it up with other players who make you play better.

Surround yourself with people who have *passionate styles:* People who know how to get excited about something and get others excited about it, too. People who channel their passions to find success. People who can build you up with the passion and knowledge needed to approach opportunities or new techniques. People who you feel make you a more passionate person just by spending an hour with them. Although you must always stay true to who you are at your core, surround yourself with people who can help you further shape your own passionate style, making it even more impressive. Ask yourself, "Who do I want in my network in 15 years?" Associate yourself with people who are passionate about life today and passionate about tomorrow.

Surround yourself with *fearless* people: People who work toward solutions when the inevitable challenges arrive. People who aren't beaten down and negative about the future. Fearless-minded people live in a world of "what if I could?" rather than a world of "what if I don't?" Fearless people always believe there is a way and don't hear the words "no" or "can't" when it comes to their future successes. Fearless people are aggressive with opportunities, but can also be creatively, uniquely, and respectfully persistent.

Surround yourself with people who have a *game plan*—people who have focus and vision, and who anticipate. Believe in having a strategy to move forward and create results. Build a network with people who have goals and embrace their opportunities to challenge themselves to do more, be more, and create more.

Finally, surround yourself with people who have proven they can *manage choices*. Those will be the people with whom you can create a mutual respect. Just as you have worked hard to manage your great choices, surround yourself with people who have been tenacious and intelligent enough to also handle the choices they created for themselves.

These five-tool players will become your friends, your clients, and your colleagues, and these people will be the network you turn to when a young person approaches you for career advice one day. Teach her these five tools and help her understand their importance. Remind her to enjoy the journey, because, as you know, it is the journey that connects you to your dream career. And most important, be sure she can answer the two simple but central questions Lonnie once asked a young adult with more passion than experience:

"Who are you? And what to do you want to do?"

The conversation is continued at www.yourdreamjobgameplan.com

Index